RESIGNATION MONDAY

A PASTOR'S GUIDE TO NOT QUITTING

TOBY LOFTON

Resignation Monday: A Pastor's Guide to NOT Quitting

PrecisionFaith.com

Cover Design by Sam Art Studio

ISBN: 9798399657035

A PrecisionFaith Devotional

BELIEF
MADE
SIMPLE

A HOLY WEEK JOURNEY
— INTO —
DISCIPLESHIP

TOBY LOFTON

Your Free Devotional Is Waiting

Searching for more meaning to Holy Week? Discover how to enrichen your belief in the one who died for your sins.

Get a free electronic copy of this special PrecisionFaith Devotional honoring the last days of Christ. Available for Kindle and e-readers, or PDF at https://dl.bookfunnel.com/deanxe7n16. Purchase a paperback version on Amazon.

Contents

PREFACE

To my co-workers in Christ,

I want to share with you a powerful prayer. It is more of a conversation—a brief dialogue between God and a man God called to lead. I believe the lessons from this exchange can transform your pastoral leadership.

The petitions to God and God's responses have changed how I approach being a pastor. They have become my guideposts to Christian leadership. More importantly, they have helped me overcome those trying days pastors often face.

If you are looking for what to do, or want to become a better pastor, join me as we explore the prayer of one of God's greatest leaders of His people.

Toby Lofton

EXODUS 33:12-34:9

12 MOSES SAID TO the Lord, "See, you have said to me, 'Bring up this people,' but you have not let me know whom you will send with me. Yet you have said, 'I know you by name, and you have also found favor in my sight.' 13 Now if I have found favor in your sight, please show me your ways, so that I may know you and find favor in your sight. Consider, too, that this nation is your people." 14 He said, "My presence will go with you, and I will give you rest." 15 And he said to him, "If your presence will not go, do not bring us up from here. 16 For how shall it be known that I have found favor in your sight, I and your people, unless you go with us? In this way, we shall be distinct, I and your people, from every people on the face of the earth."

17 The Lord said to Moses, "I will also do this thing that you have asked, for you have found favor in my sight, and I know you by name." 18 Moses said, "Please show me your glory." 19 And he said, "I will make all my goodness pass before you and will proclaim before you the name, 'The Lord,' and I will be gracious to whom I will be gracious and will show mercy on whom I will show mercy. 20 But," he said, "you cannot see my face, for no one shall see me and live." 21 And the Lord continued, "See, there is a place by me where you shall stand on the rock, 22 and while my glory passes by I will put you in a cleft of the rock, and I will cover you with my hand until I have passed by; 23 then I will take away my hand, and you shall see my back, but my face shall not be seen."

34 The Lord said to Moses, "Cut two tablets of stone like the former ones, and I will write on the tablets the words that were on the former tablets, which you broke. 2 Be ready in the morning and come up in the morning to Mount Sinai and present yourself there to me on the top of the mountain. 3 No one shall come up with you, and do not let anyone be seen throughout all the mountain, and do not let flocks or herds graze in front of that mountain." 4 So Moses cut two tablets of stone like the former ones, and

he rose early in the morning and went up on Mount Sinai, as the Lord had commanded him, and took in his hand the two tablets of stone. 5 The Lord descended in the cloud and stood with him there and proclaimed the name, "The Lord." 6 The Lord passed before him and proclaimed,

"The Lord, the Lord,

a God merciful and gracious,

slow to anger,

and abounding in steadfast love and faithfulness,

7 keeping steadfast love for the thousandth generation,

forgiving iniquity and transgression and sin,

yet by no means clearing the guilty,

but visiting the iniquity of the parents

upon the children

and the children's children

to the third and the fourth generation."

8 And Moses quickly bowed down to the ground and worshiped. 9 He said, "If now I have found favor in your sight, my Lord, I pray, let my Lord go with us. Although this is a stiff-necked people, pardon our iniquity and our sin, and take us for your inheritance."

1

RESIGNATION MONDAY

THERE YOU ARE. SITTING at your desk first thing on Monday morning.

It's not just any Monday. Today is Resignation Monday.

Resignation Monday isn't a holiday. It is not a day of celebration. It is a day of dread.

For some pastors, Resignation Monday doesn't occur often. For others, Resignation Monday can be a common occasion, almost every Monday.

Come Monday morning, just hours after Sunday worship services, you walk into your office, open the top drawer, and take out your pre-written resignation letter. You read it over and over, wondering if it is time to quit?

On other Mondays, you place the letter in front of you on your desk. You place your elbows on the desk, head in hand, running your hands through your hair and you wonder, "How long can I keep doing this?"

Yep, that's the Monday. If you have been there, you know.

Sometimes Resignation Monday makes little sense. You have no reason to be contemplating resigning. Yesterday's worship service was great. You could see the people responding to your message. Lots of head nods, some Amens even. People may have been clapping. No complaining. No bickering. It would seem like your ministry is doing well.

Yet, come Monday morning, one would think your congregation booed and threw rotten tomatoes at you during the service. One might suspect the deacons escorted you out of the building, telling you never to return.

None of that happened, of course. The fact is, you don't know what happened. Yet there you are. Resignation letter in hand. "I can't do this anymore!"

Sometimes Resignation Monday makes sense. No one would question why you sit where you are today. Sunday may have been the same ole same ole. No one responding to the Holy Spirit. Glazed over eyes staring at you while you preached. You may have seen some piercing looks. If looks

5

could kill, you'd be dead right there behind the pulpit. Your words seemed to fall on people who cannot hear. Nothing wrong with their ears, other than they have stopped them. They chose not to listen.

You may be tired of the bickering as well. A church member may have bombarded you just moments before yesterday's worship. They complained about something in the church. Of all times, they must talk to the pastor about these issues. Why do they do it right before you preach? Couldn't it wait?

"Oh preacher, I just thought you should know."

You get that. What were you supposed to do about it right before you stepped into the pulpit?

If you have been in this business long, you know what I am talking about. Some rookies know it as well.

So yes, I get it, and so do most of your fellow pastors. Head in hand. Fingers pulling hair. You're so frustrated right now you are thinking of what you will do next. You may have already searched the web for other job opportunities. Maybe you'll go to another church? Maybe not? You are not sure you want to pastor ever again?

Resignation Monday indeed.

Here's the good news: "God is our refuge and strength, a very present help in trouble" (Psalm 46:1).

I believe God provides help through his word. I believe God's Word provides truths, examples, and stories that were written to help us in our need.

Years ago, I came across a prayer in the Bible that I think can help us through Resignation Monday. It's not so much a prayer as it is a conversation between God and Moses. Moses isn't thinking about quitting, but he understands unless God acts, all else is useless.

I don't know about you, but when Resignation Monday comes my way, I need God to act and act fast. Otherwise, I'm left wondering if it's worth it.

After twenty-five years in ministry, I've been where you are more than once. I've been there with my church, my denomination, and other ministries I worked with. I've complained to other pastors, refused to go to the office, and even stopped taking phone calls. I've taken long walks, distracted myself with other passions, and even acted out a time or two.

I know what it is like to search for answers. I also know what it is like to search in all the wrong places for the answer. One thing I have learned is God is the only place our answer rests. So if we are asking what to do, God is our first stop.

God's Word records a conversation between Moses and God. This conversation has helped me on more than one occasion. I believe it can help regain your focus and get back on a track with God.

I suggest if you apply the principles of this prayer to your current situation, you can find the strength to not quit. Even if you resign, you will have a better understanding of the course you have taken, other than just being mad and frustrated with your church.

Even if you are not facing Resignation Monday, the lessons learned through Moses' prayer are profound. They can change your relationship with God and your people. I've even learned to make this prayer part of my daily routine as I seek to lead God's people. While I have used this prayer for discernment, it has become a tool for spiritual growth. The verses containing Moses' prayer are packed with God's truths.

So come along. Let's lean on Moses as he teaches us to lean on God. Let's see if the Moses' prayer can help us overcome Resignation Monday, or just make us a better Christian.

2

TALK TO THE RIGHT PERSON

Now Moses used to take the tent and pitch
it outside the camp, far off from the camp;
he called it the tent of meeting. And everyone
who sought the Lord would go out to the
tent of meeting, which was outside the camp.
Whenever Moses went out to the tent, all the
people would rise and stand, each of them, at
the entrance of their tents and watch Moses
until he had gone into the tent. When Moses
entered the tent, the pillar of cloud would
descend and stand at the entrance of the tent,

and the Lord would speak with Moses. When all the people saw the pillar of cloud standing at the entrance of the tent, all the people would rise and bow down, all of them, at the entrance of their tent. Thus the Lord used to speak to Moses face to face, as one speaks to a friend.

Exodus 33:7-11

Your Tent of Meeting

I SUSPECT THAT IF you are staring at your resignation letter, or contemplating one, you are in the place you engage God most. For many pastors, that is in their office. It is in the place where they turn to God.

In that moment when we are thinking about hanging up our guns, we don't realize it's a holy place. But it is true. For most of us, when Resignation Monday hits us, we are somewhere God's presence is most meaningful to us. That makes it holy.

We contemplate in places that help us contemplate. When it comes time to center ourselves with God, we find a setting where we can do that.

A friend of mine built a cabin in the spot God called him to ministry. He would often go there when he was struggling in ministry or had major decisions to make. The cabin was his go-to place when he needed to spend deep time with God.

An elderly church member had a garden, complete with a prayer bench. She had several benches in the garden, but her prayer bench was significant. It is where she met with God every morning, reserved only for that purpose.

While I was traveling frequently, I found the place God spoke with me most was on airplanes. There, in the humming silence of a jet, nowhere for me to go, nothing else for me to do, God and I had some of our deepest conversations.

We go to these places because God draws us there. They provide the ambience for us to experience God most. We go there because we sense God.

For reasons beyond us, God chooses special places to converse with us. I believe God chooses where he meets with us the most. Sure, we can have those casual talks anywhere. But when it is serious business time, God reserves that work for special places.

Moses met with God in the Tent of Meeting. Bethel was significant for Jacob. Daniel had a room where he went to pray. Jesus went to the Mount of Olives. The disciples gathered in the upper room. God chooses special places we can encounter him the most.

In every pastorate I have served, God has chosen such places for me. In one church, my special place was kneeling by two chairs that were in my church office. My deepest conversations with God occurred early in the morning or late at night. Currently, my Tent of Meeting is in my home office, even though I have a church office. For reasons I don't question, God speaks to me most often in my home office.

God has a special place for you. Find your special place if you don't know where it is. I bet you have one. You just may not be aware of it. Sometimes it might not be a specific place per se, rather a condition.

I'm convinced, like Moses, Daniel, the disciples, and Jesus, we have a special place to meet with God.

Go to the place you encounter God if you are experiencing Resignation Monday. Get there as quickly as you can. Get to the place God has chosen for you to meet.

Who Are You Talking To?

When we are considering resigning, we aren't thinking about God. We're not. Even though we cry out to God, we concentrate on our misery. We are thinking about ourselves. We might think about the people causing us this misery. But we are not thinking about God.

Too often, we only have the "I've had it" conversation with ourselves. In our pity party, and it is a pity, and that is not derogatory, often we only converse with ourselves. Sometimes we converse with the people we blame, and they're not even present. Most often, we talk to ourselves. We are not talking to God.

"Oh, I was crying to God. My spirit was."

Maybe? But not likely. Not if we are honest. We hold this conversation about moving on only with ourselves. Nobody else is present. Oh sure, God is there. God is everywhere. We know. But you still aren't talking to God. No. This is a conversation you are having with you.

One of our arguments with ourselves as we debate Resignation Monday is "Why me?" We ask this in many forms. Notice how the questions aren't directed to anyone but yourself.

13

"Why me?"

"Why did I do this?"

"What was I thinking?"

"Why did I choose this?"

"Why did I leave a promising career to come into the ministry?"

Sometimes we look for blame. "What did I do to deserve this?"

"How come they are treating me this way?"

Then we question our own faithfulness.

"Did I sin?"

"Have I done something wrong?"

We question our calling. "Did God really call me?"

"Was I truly called?"

Heaven forbids if we answer ourselves, especially if Satan enters the conversation. Let's remember, Satan is called the great deceiver for a reason.

If you want to have the "I'm quitting" conversation, have it with God. You have talked with God before. Conversing with God now shouldn't be anything different. You have talked with God in many places. Driving down the road. In your house. At a restaurant. In your bedroom. At a class meeting. In seminary. I would hope that you have conversed with God every week that you have preached. Talking with God isn't anything new to you.

If you are going to have a resignation conversation, get to your special place as quickly as you can. You're going to your secret place to talk with God. You are not going there to talk to anyone else, including yourself. You are going to converse with the Holy.

Why Talk with God

It shows when we spend time with God. Compare a pastor that doesn't spend time with God with one who does. The one who spends time with God will stand out. It is clear they have spent time with God. The way they talk, the things they say, how they act, how they carry themselves, all reveal they have spent time with God.

It is possible to be a successful pastor without a connection to God. You can do it, and many have. There are pastors with successful ministries that don't spend time with God. They are people persons. People like them. They can preach. Their eloquence in speaking about their sermon topic is remarkable. They are committed Christians. However, there is a difference between a person who spends time with God and one who does not, no matter how successful their ministry appears. Success, however, will not get rid of Resignation Monday.

I once interviewed a denominational leader. This leader guided new church growth and revitalization in his denomination. He got this position because he was in love with God and his ministry blossomed. Years into his leadership, I went to discuss how his spirituality had led him to become who he was. As I inquired about his faith, he evaded the question by talking about all the growth in his denomination and what they were preparing to do. I finally stopped him, telling him I didn't come to hear about denominational planning. I came to discuss how his spirituality had influenced his work. He became silent as tears streamed down his eyes. We sat there for a good five minutes as he wept. After composing himself, he confessed he had put so much time and energy on church growth that he had lost touch with the One who had inspired him to pursue church growth.

One principle you will hear repeated throughout this book is your relationship with God is important. It's a biblical principle found in several biblical leaders. The bible provides stories revealing what happens when a person has a relationship with God and what happens when they don't.

The only reason you are going to your special place to talk with God is because you have a relationship with God. The words describing Moses' conversations with God state it best:

Thus the Lord used to speak to Moses face to face, as one speaks to a friend (Exodus 33:11)

You are entering your Tent of Meeting to talk to your friend. Your friend, by the way, is the key to how you handle Resignation Monday. Your relationship with God is the secret.

Go Ahead—Complain!

Resignation Monday often revolves around complaining. Either you're complaining or your people are complaining. We do not confine complaining to words. We complain in many forms. Some complain by saying something. Others complain by not saying anything. There are those who complain using their expressions, facial and body. Others complain through their actions. Complaining doesn't go hidden. We can see it.

Let's start with our people first. Let's discuss how they complain and what they often complain about. We'll put it in context first. So, you are a pastor. The church appointed, hired, or called you, however you prefer to look at it. Regardless, you are the pastor of a church.

Normally, a pastor is a stranger to the church they are in. Exceptions exist, but rarely do pastors serve in their home church. Pastors don't serve where they grew up in the nursery. We don't serve in places we have worshiped all our lives. Most pastors serve in communities and churches where they have never been before.

A pastor's identity is often one of the first challenges faced when trying to lead a church. Here you are, preaching the word of God, encouraging your people into mission and ministry. You see things differently from your church. As an outsider, you can identify growth points. You can point out areas that need improvement. You see habits that need to be addressed. Valid reasons may exist why they operate the way they do. As an outsider, you may not know those reasons. They may have tried to work on those areas before, but failed. Yet, as you lead, leaning on these pressure points, one of the first things that will come up is your identity. Who are you to tell them what to do? You have only been there a short time. They have been there all their lives.

Often it does not matter that you have proven to be devout. Your sermons could be God-inspired-spirit-filled.

You may be the best preacher they ever have heard and your care for your people is exceptional. The church may have grown numerically and spiritually. Signs and wonders abound. But press one of those hot buttons and you are an outsider.

A seasoned pastor once told me I would always be an outsider. Like Moses, who was of the same flesh and blood, was an outsider. Moses grew up in the palace. He was the one who killed another person. Moses left Egypt. He was the stranger that showed up from nowhere. Moses even had a foreign wife. While they grew to love Moses, Moses was an outsider.

Your people are going to complain. It doesn't matter how well the church functions. They will find something to complain about. Sometimes, they complain because the church is doing so well.

Think about a dirty window. Smudges and smears, dirt and grime are visible all over it. People note the window is dirty, but they don't point out anything specific about it being dirty. Clean the window now and allow a child to put a handprint on it. Everyone will point out the handprint. The rest of the window is clean. They see the handprint. One reason they see the hand smudge is because it stands out in a crystal-clear window. When all the window is dirty, a single smudge isn't visible. It just blends in with the rest. Little Johnny, putting his hand on the window, will not matter. Let the window be spotless. Little Johnny better not get near that window. Heaven forbids if he does. If little Johnny puts his hand on the window, we'll never hear the end until we remove his handprint. Anybody and everybody are going to point it out.

The church is similar. Problems and issues stand out when the church is thriving. People see the problems and then they complain about them.

I once pastored a church that had made great strides in mission and ministry. A lady complained to me about a problem. It was not just a problem. It was a twenty-year-old problem. After she shared me with me her complaint, I inquired about how long this had been a problem.

"Twenty years," she stated.

"So why now?" I asked. "Why bring this up now?"

"I thought since everything was going so well, we could fix this problem."

"Let me get this straight. Because everything is going so well right now, you want to discuss a twenty-year-old problem? A problem the church has said they can do ministry without it?"

Another complaint often voiced in the church, "We haven't done it that way before."

Of course, you haven't. It's called a new thing.

When facing hardships and God's call for sacrifice, the simplest complaint is the desire to revert to the way things used to be. "We didn't have these issues when that ministry didn't exist."

Correct, you didn't. Because that ministry didn't exist. But now you have this ministry, and it brings with it added challenges that must addressed.

Here's the thing about people. People complain. A military commander once told a group of younger leaders that when their people stopped complaining, they needed to become concerned. Something was wrong.

Another commander I served with used to say soldiers complain. That's just what they do. Make everything right for them. Address every complaint they voice. They'll still find something to complain about.

Pastors complain too. We complain to God. We complain to ourselves. Our spouses get to hear us complain. Our fellow pastors get to listen. People within our inner circle listen as well. We complain and often in the same unproductive ways as our church members sometimes do.

21

I can't tell you how many times I have heard pastors call their churches names like "the frozen chosen," "heathens," and "deadbeats." I once moved to a new community to pastor a new church. The pastors met for lunch once a month. They invited me to join them. As soon as we gathered, they started lambasting their churches. The entire meal that I stayed for was nothing more than bashing their people. Apparently, one of them noticed my silence. "Oh, you just wait. Your church is going to do this. Your people do not differ from our people." I stayed for about thirty minutes and excused myself. I did not attend another pastor gathering.

I have had my moments as well. I have complained to my pastoral friends and even to God on more than one occasion. Moses complained as well. He was no stranger to complaining. Moses even complained to God because his people were complaining to him. I suppose that is the irony of the cycle of complaining. Our people complain, so we complain. We complain, so our people complain.

Complaining isn't always a bad thing. Complaining is useful if it leads to a solution. When you are the one being complained about, it can be painful, like Resignation Monday painful. Yet, good can result if you address the complaint.

We have been taught complaining is bad. We have been told there is no need to complain. Nobody will listen anyway. Neither are true. Complaining for the sake of complaining is a problem. Complaining to find a solution is not.

The problem with the church, like Moses' people, is they often complain for the sake of complaining. Nobody attempts to find a solution. They just complain.

"Water is bitter."

"Food is not available."

"We don't have any water."

"Nobody is in charge."

"There's no deity to worship."

Productive complaining acknowledges the problem while seeking a solution. Productive complaining provides a resolution to the complaint. By modeling and teaching productive complaining, we can impede the unhealthy complaint cycle.

Let's face it: A key source that leads to Resignation Monday is complaining, ours and our people. Complaints, disgruntling, and grumbling influence the Monday morning review of the resignation letter. How we handle it determines what happens next. The prayer of Moses can help us move beyond complaining and lead us into healthy congregational leadership that can influence our people.

Let's change the dread of Resignation Monday. Let's take what once made us want to quit and turn it into effective, productive congregational leadership. The thing about congregational leadership is that it starts with us.

3

REMEMBER

"See, you have said to me, 'Bring up this
people,' but you have not let me know
whom you will send with me. Yet you have
said, 'I know you by name, and you have
also found favor in my sight.'"

Exodus 33:12

REMEMBER WHO YOU ARE. Before you do anything
or say anything, remember. You are not just going to
remember who you are; you are going to remember
whose you are.

One problem of Resignation Monday is we forget who we are and whose we are. The first step is to recompose ourselves in our proper position in a relationship with God before we complain about our situation. We do that by remembering four truths.

God Called You

> See, you have said to me, 'Bring up this
> people,'

Start your conversation with God by reminding yourself, and even God, that you are called. While we will get to our ministry calling, Casey Cole reminds us we are first called to be disciples of Jesus[1]

One of the most important things you can do is remember you are a disciple of Christ first. In fact, you were a disciple of Jesus before you were called to ministry. Remember, you are a disciple.

---

1. Casey Cole, OFM. Called: What Happens After Saying Yes to God (Cincinnati: Franciscan Media, 2018) 206.

We define discipleship as one who adheres to the doctrines of another and spreads those doctrines. As a Christian disciple, you are one who adheres to the doctrine of Jesus and you spread those teachings. You do not need to be a pastor to be obedient and share your faith. Every Christian is called to do these.

Put the resignation letter aside for now. Focus on the basics first. Go to God as God's child before approaching God as a church leader. Start by thinking about your relationship with Jesus as a disciple.

Recall your personal testimony of coming to know Jesus as your Lord and Savior. Spend some time working through this. Don't rush through it.

For many people, their story isn't a onetime event. Their story begins with being brought up in the church, raised by Christian parents.

Others may have a onetime transformation testimony, like the Apostle Paul's Damascus Road experience. There was more to Paul's salvation story than that bright, shining light. Paul was a devout Jew before Jesus blinded him. Think about your life before Jesus. When did you come to know him? When did you commit to follow Jesus?

You may also want to remember your journey with Jesus as you walked along the way as a disciple. Recall the church that helped mature your faith. Think about the pastors, teachers, mentors, and others that supported and encouraged your Christian walk. Think about how you spread the teachings of Jesus and those that you have influenced for Christ.

Remember, you are a child of God, regardless of your leadership position or anything else surrounding the church. Dick Wills reminds in Waking to God's Dream, "Joy comes from walking with God and is not dependent on external circumstances."[2] Set aside the external circumstances of your church. Recall where your joy comes from.

As you reflect upon your calling as a disciple, assess your walk with Christ. As hard as it may be, remove yourself from your professional role and think of yourself only as a Christian.

How is your Christian walk? How has your relationship been with Jesus Christ? Have you been a faithful disciple? Have you adhered to his teachings? Are you spreading the doctrines of Christ? Can you call others to follow Christ

---

2. Dick Wills. Waking to God's Dream: Spiritual Leadership and Church Renewal (Nashville: Abingdon, 1999) 32.

and spread his doctrine if you are not doing it yourself? Can you point out the faults of others if you are not adhering to Jesus' teaching?

Remove yourself from the church and think about your own spiritual walk with Christ. Recall the joy you felt. Remember what it meant to be a Christian, loved, saved, and cared for by Jesus. Reflect on the mercy, grace, and forgiveness you received. Talk with God about your experience. Express your thankfulness to him. You may realize that somehow, along the way of being a pastor, you have forgotten what being saved meant. It's possible you've been acting more like a pastor than a Christian, or more like a CEO than a child of God.

While this is not our focus in this section, it is connected to Resignation Monday in two specific ways. One, you must have a faithful relationship with God. Two, your faithfulness has a direct correlation with your people.

The Apostle John taught, God first loved you (1 John 4:19).

Before you fret about anything, remember God loves you. God loves you and gave his Son Jesus for you. God saved you through the cross. You are called like God calls every Christian. You are a child of God.

Called Again

> See, you have said to me, 'Bring up this
> people.'

Those were the words of Moses. We have identified this as Moses' calling. Moses wasn't afraid to remind God about what God had said. He wasn't afraid to remind God of his calling. This wasn't just Moses telling God to remember however, Moses remembered as well. Moses was familiar with his encounter with God at the burning bush and the call to set his people free.

You have been called as well. You have been called to pastor.

Remember your calling to ministry. Where were you? What happened? How did you know? How did you hear God? What were the events leading up to your call? During your call? Following your call?

A good practice I have used over the years is to rewrite my calling. I write my call story just as I did when I submitted it to my Board of Ministry. The more I rewrite it, the more insight God gives me to what he called me to do. I also find the power of the calling rekindled and strengthened.

The purpose of having you remember your calling is to reconnect you to that calling. Not only are we short-sighted to our Christian testimony, but our calling can become distant as well. When we are struggling, we can forget our calling.

Questioning your calling is okay. Author Casey Cole, speaking about his own experience, writes, "Discernment of God's will is not a matter of finite, ready-to-complete-and-move-on decisions, but an ongoing process of constantly requesting God's assistance each and every day."[3]

Your calling isn't a onetime conversation, rather one that extends across time, months, years, even. You have a continuous calling and must discern your calling often.

If, after reflecting upon your calling and discerning it yet again, you, without question, know you were called, you can rip your resignation up, at least the part of quitting the ministry altogether.

Do not base your calling on the current situation in your church. Your calling has nothing to do with your people

---

3. Casey Cole, OFM. Called: What Happens After Saying Yes to God (Cincinnati: Franciscan Media, 2018) 199.

responding to the message. Your call doesn't involve the number of complaints or compliments you get from your people.

God didn't say, "Go be a pastor. I only called you if things go great. If they don't go great, then I never called you." You were called before you were a pastor. You answered the call before receiving a church. Your church has nothing to do with your calling.

Most leaders called by God in the Bible faced challenges. You are in splendid company. God called one of the greatest prophets in history to carry a message to the people. After giving Isaiah his message, God told him the people would not listen. Your calling has nothing to do with the response of the people. Your calling is about God saying to you, "Bring up this people."

The vision God provided Peter while he was praying on the roof of his house provides an excellent principle we can apply. God showed Peter a blanket with all kinds of animals, clean and unclean. God told Peter to kill and eat. Since eating unclean food was against Jewish traditions, Peter refused. Two more times, God insisted and Peter refused.

After the men sent by Cornelius, a Gentile, arrived, requesting Peter to share the gospel with them, Peter understood the principle—if God has said it, so be it.

If God has called you, you are called. That settles it. Remember your calling from God and rejoice.

God is With You

>...you have not let me know whom you will send with me.

One of the loneliest feeling a pastor can experience is sitting at a desk contemplating giving up. It feels lonely because we feel lonely. We may even have an inner circle of supporters, those on our side. Yet we feel like no one is with us. New people joining the church, faces lighting up as you preach, but come Resignation Monday, you're alone. That's just how it feels.

Let's say that again. That's just how it feels. Did you hear that? It is a feeling. It is a feeling and nothing else.

According to the scriptures, you are not alone. You have the most powerful presence in the universe with you. God is with you, just as he promised. Not only is God with you, but Jesus is also with you. And to make sure you don't miss their presence, the Holy Spirit is with you.

As a follower of Jesus Christ, one who keeps the teachings of Jesus and spreads them, God, Jesus, and the Holy Spirit are with you. Forget about being a pastor for a moment. The word of God says this to every believer.

> "If you love me, you will keep my commandments. And I will ask the Father, and he will give you another Advocate, to be with you forever. This is the Spirit of truth, whom the world cannot receive because it neither sees him nor knows him. You know him because he abides with you, and he will be in you.

> "I will not leave you orphaned; I am coming to you. In a little while the world will no longer see me, but you will see me; because I live, you also will live. On that day you will know that I am in my Father, and you in me, and I in you. They who have my commandments and keep them are those who love me, and those who love me will be loved by my Father, and I will love them and reveal myself to them."

Jesus answered him, "Those who love me will keep my word, and my Father will love them, and we will come to them and make our home with them.

"I have said these things to you while I am still with you. But the Advocate, the Holy Spirit, whom the Father will send in my name, will teach you everything and remind you of all that I have said to you. Peace I leave with you; my peace I give to you. I do not give to you as the world gives. Do not let your hearts be troubled, and do not let them be afraid.

John 14:15-21, 23, 25-27

If you are a believer in Jesus, and obedient to Jesus, God, and Christ dwell within you. Christ has also sent the Holy Spirit to be with you. As Jesus taught, as his disciple, you are never alone.

If you are thinking, "It doesn't feel like it. I feel alone." Don't worry, so did Moses.

In the prayer of Moses, Moses said, "You haven't told me who would go with me."

The irony of Moses' claim is that God had told Moses. Not only had God told him, Moses and the people witnessed God's presence.

God had told Moses who he was going to send with him. He had done this in a variety of ways and forms. He told Moses that he would be his mouth and teach him what to say (Exodus 4:12). After Moses tried to get out of it, he told Moses he would send Aaron with him (Exodus 4:14-16). When God delivered the Israelites from Egypt, he went before them as a pillar of cloud by day and a pillar of fire by night, never leaving them. When God parted the Red Sea, the angel of God and the pillar of cloud moved from in front of them to behind them to protect them from the Egyptian army. Even the Egyptians understood God was present fighting on Israel's behalf. From the mountain Moses received the Law, God told Moses that he was sending an angel in front of them, to guard them, and bring them to the place prepared for them. God's name was in the angel (23:20-33).

Moses wasn't the only servant of God to feel alone. Elijah once thought he was the only one left. After a seemingly incredible victory over Jezebel, her prophets, and Baal, Elijah is ready to give up. He sits under a tree, depressed.

Elijah complains to God that he is the only prophet left. God informs Elijah he had 7,000 loyal followers. The irony of the story is Elijah was never alone. God had always been with Elijah as apparent at the latest victory, and the many other miracles Elijah performed. In fact, God's presence is greater than any number of followers.

Like Moses and Elijah, we forget about God's presence in tough and trying times. Know this, however, you are not alone.

God Knows You

Yet you have said, 'I know you by name…'

God knows you. You are not just a number on a roster. You are not just one of many millions of Christians who have followed Jesus. God knows you.

Jesus taught God knows the number of hairs on your head (Luke 12:7).

The prophet Jeremiah claimed God knew him before he was ever born (Jeremiah 1:5). Many interpret Jeremiah's claim as applicable to everyone.

The very nature of your calling shows how well God knows humanity. Recall what God said when he called Moses: "I have seen them. I have heard their cries" (Exodus 3:7).

God knows us so well that when Cain killed Abel, Abel's blood called out to God. God heard it (Genesis 4:10).

When Moses was on the mountain, God let Moses know the people were rebelling down below. It was God who told Moses they were building a false god.

Your plight, your crying out to God, isn't fresh news to him. God knows it. He knows how you feel.

In all its tenses in the Bible, to know someone means an intimate knowledge of them. There is more to knowing someone than knowing who they are. God knows you intimately.

God knows how you are feeling right now. He knows your struggles. God knows how your people are acting. He knows if it is one, two, or the entire church that is giving you a fit. You are that known by God.

God Favors You

> Yet you have said, '...you have also found
> favor in my sight.'

God favors you. You have gained God's favor.

Having God's favor is a bold statement. While it is true God loves everyone, God does not favor everyone. We must meet terms and conditions to gain God's favor.

We learn from the Bible conditions exist to gain God's favor.

> Do not let loyalty and faithfulness forsake
> you; bind them around your neck; write
> them on the tablet of your heart. Then you
> will find favor and high regard in the sight
> of God and of people.
>
> Proverbs 3:3-4

> For this finds favor, if for the sake of
> conscience toward God a person bears up
> under sorrows when suffering unjustly.
>
> 1 Peter 2:19

The Bible also provides examples of people who gained God's favor.

> But Noah found favor in the eyes of the Lord.
>
> Genesis 6:8

> Now the boy Samuel was growing in stature
> and in favor, both with the Lord and with
> men.
>
> 1 Samuel 2:26

> David found favor in God's sight and asked
> that he might find a dwelling place for the
> God of Jacob.
>
> Acts 7:46

The angel said to her, "Do not be afraid,
Mary; for you have found favor with God."

Luke 1:30

And Jesus kept increasing in wisdom and
stature, and in favor with God and men.

Luke 2:5

People in the Bible that gained the favor of God lived righteous and just lives. God does not favor everyone.

We aren't told the details of Moses' faithfulness to God. We are told his birth story, what happened at his birth. We learn about his upbringing. The story of Moses helping a Jewish slave is given to us. He ran away and by chance came across his future wife, who he then helped. We read his call narrative at the burning bush followed by the story of the Exodus event, but that is all we know about Moses.

We could deduce that because of Moses' obedience to God's call, he had found favor. Moses seems to measure up to the expectations and examples of God's favor, as we saw in the scriptures.

Without question, however, God called Moses to be more than he was. God drew him out to something more. God drew him out to draw others out. It was his calling. It was who he was. Because of his willingness to do it, God favored Moses.

Your faithfulness to God, your relationship with Jesus, affects the promise of God's favor. For you to be favored by God, you must live your life as Jesus teaches.

Your relationship with God is the most important consideration involving your leadership. Lewis Park and Bruce Birch point out in their book about David's leadership that David's success was based on his intimate relationship with God. When the relationship broke down, so did David's leadership.[4]

Are you favored by God? Are you living your life in the favor of God?

Gaining favor has nothing to do with your salvation. We cannot gain our salvation. Salvation is a gift of God given to us through Jesus Christ. However, salvation is not a licensed to live in rebellion to God's purposes for you.

---

4. Lewis A. Parks and Bruce C. Birch. Ducking Spears, Dancing Madly: A Biblical Model of Church Leadership (Nashville: Abingdon, 2004).

I wish I could tell you with certainty that God favors you. I can't do that, however. Only the Lord and you know if you have obediently followed Jesus.

I can tell you this: if you obey Jesus Christ, imitate God's ways, and answer your calling to pastoral leadership, God will favor you.

Obedience is crucial. If you haven't obeyed Jesus, Resurrection Monday is the least of your concerns right now. Stop worrying about whether to quit. Spend time with Jesus. Your struggle may be more about faithfulness than it does anything in your church.

On the other hand, if you know you have been obedient, you have been loyal and faithful, then you can know God favors you. Rest in this knowledge. Resignation Monday isn't about your faithfulness.

We've remembered four things in this chapter. God called us. God is with us. God knows us. God favors us. These four things alone provide strength and encouragement to continue being who God called us. Yet, there is more that we need to do.

PRECISION**F**AITH **R**ECAP

LET'S DO A RECAP. Recaps are spread throughout the book to remember the principles discovered in Moses' conversation with God. They can provide an outline of talking points to use when you are speaking with God as well.

1. You are experiencing Resignation Monday.

2. Run to your place of meeting, the place you sense God the most.

3. You know you need to talk to God.

4. God's Word reminds you are his child.

5. God called you to pastor before sending you to

lead.

6. God is with you.

4

WANT GOD'S WAYS

Now if I have found favor in your sight,
please show me your ways, so that I may
know you and find favor in your sight.
Consider, too, that this nation is your
people.

Exodus 33:13

ONE PERIL OF MINISTRY, or even your relationship
with God, is contentment. Often, we become content in
our intimacy with God. Sometimes we don't mean to, it
just happens.

As pastors, we can get so caught up with doing ministry we forget about the one who sent us into ministry. We can get so worried about the church that we forget to whom the church belongs. We can also become so focused on ourselves that everything becomes about us, rather than Jesus.

My doctoral research revealed most pastors spend less time with God after they enter the ministry than they did when they first entered the ministry. Many reported not talking with God daily. Some did not pray except during worship or small group meetings. Others reported only reading the Bible to prepare for the Sunday Sermon. When queried more about their relationship with God, the responses were disheartening.

Resignation Monday can be a wake-up call. Maybe the issue isn't the church. Maybe the issue is us. Perhaps we place too much weight regarding our happiness on how well our churches are doing. Maybe God uses the church to guide us towards true happiness. Perhaps we base our happiness on our relationship with the church rather than God. So, God challenges our relationship with our church to redirect our focus to our relationship with Him.

While we may have a relationship with God, Moses teaches us having a relationship isn't enough. Moses wasn't content with merely knowing God. He wasn't content with being Israel's spiritual leader or God's promised presence. Moses desired more.

Want to Know God's Ways

Please show me your ways...

Moses wanted to know God's ways for three reasons. He understood knowing God's ways would help him know God more. Moses knew the closer he followed God's ways, the more God would favor him. He also knew the more favor he had, the better leader he would be for God's people.

Having a relationship with someone involves more than just knowing someone's origin, occupation, preferences, and dislikes. If you want to really know someone, you will need to know more than those things. What you really want is to understand their ways. You want to know how they do things. It is their actions that identify who they are.

A person's identity isn't based upon their birthplace, family, how tall they are, how short they are, red hair, brown hair, blue or green eyes, what kind of car they drive, and so on. Their identity is based on their motives, what drives them, the rationale for their actions. Actions reveal identity. Knowing this is key to building a relationship.

Often, when we turn to God, we don't seek to know God. What we want is for God to tell us what to do. This is particularly true on Resignation Monday. We turn to God. "God, tell me what to do. Do I quit? Do I resign? Find another job? Should I buckle under pressure and do as they ask?" That's where we start. It's the wrong place to start.

The right place is by asking God to show you his ways. It's the popular adage of "What Would Jesus Do?" You are asking, "God, what would you do in my situation?"

I suggest an even better place to start is simply to put the factors you can't control aside and work on your relationship with God instead. The one thing you have absolute control over is your relationship with God. You can grow closer to God, gain more favor with God, and increase your awareness of his presence.

What's interesting is that the stronger your relationship with God, the less you must ask God what he would do. You will know God so well that you will already know what God would do. Your task is merely to follow God's ways.

Jesus told his disciples he was going to the Father. He also told them they knew how to get there. This left the disciples dumbfounded.

"What do you mean, we know the way? Show us the way."

"That's what I have been doing," Jesus replied. "You see the Father when you look at me. I am the way. Do what I have shown you. Do what I have done."

The prophets Isaiah and Micah said nations and people will come and say, "Come, let us go up to the mountain of the Lord, to the house of the God of Jacob; that He may teach us concerning his ways and that we may walk in his paths" (Isaiah 2:3/Micah 4:2).

Look to God's example for handling any situation, religious or not. Once you know how God handles it, you will know how you are to handle it. Stop asking God to tell you what to do. Observe God's actions and you will know.

Know God More

...so that I may know you

Moses wanted to know God. Moses wanted to understand God. Maybe Moses was seeking to answer why. Why was God doing this? What was God's intention to call me? Why did he draw us out? He finds the answer through knowing God better.

You want to know God's ways so that you can know God more. It's all about building your relationship with God. You want a closer walk with God. You want a deeper understanding of God.

Jesus said, "Do not let your hearts be troubled. Believe in God; believe also in me" (John 14:1).

To believe in a person, we must know them. Jesus taught eternal life is about knowing God and his Son (John 17:3). Believing in Jesus is about a relationship, not acknowledging he died on the cross. His death is part of it, but what God seeks is a relationship with us.

God's desire for a relationship is clear throughout the Bible. The Creation story tells of God walking with Adam and Eve in the garden. Exodus speaks of God desiring to be amid the people, first in the Tabernacle, then in the Temple. The prophets spoke of God placing the Law in their minds and write it in their hearts so the people would know Him. The birth of Christ is about God dwelling with us. Jesus promised he and his father would make their residence within us with the Holy Spirit. And, the last triumph of the Revelations is that God dwells with his people. God desires to be with us and for us to know him—to be in a relationship.

As we established already, knowing random details about a person doesn't help us know them. It gives us basic information, but in the spirit of the Bible, it does not help us have an intimate relationship with them. For that to happen, we must understand more about who they are, meaning their personality, their values, and their beliefs. We want to understand their way of doing. By understanding their ways, we get to know them more.

To know God better, one must comprehend his ways. Perhaps the lesson here for us is to shift our focus from ourselves, our plight, our misery, and dwell upon getting to know God more.

The answer to our resignation question hinges on knowing more about God. The more we know of God, the more we discover what God would do in our situation, how he handles our situation, and thus how we should handle our situation.

Want More Favor

so that I may... find favor in your sight.

The second reason Moses asked God to show him his ways was so that Moses could gain more favor with God. Of course, the route to gaining more favor goes through improving his relationship with God. The path to improve a relationship with God is getting to know God more. Understanding God's ways is key to knowing him better.

The more we understand God's ways, the more we get to know God. The more we know God, the stronger our relationship grows. As our relationship strengthens, we gain more favor with God. Why? We follow God's example in our actions. When we do things in the ways God does things, it pleases God.

Consider:

God created us in his image (Genesis 1:26-27). Our identity and actions should reflect God's.

Scriptures teach us to be holy as God is holy (Leviticus 11:44). Be and do the things God does.

Jesus told us to be perfect as our Father in heaven is perfect (Matthew 5:48). Again, be and do.

God's teachings, including those by Jesus, reflect his actions.

Jesus said, "I do nothing that my father doesn't do. I do the same works of God" (John 5:19-20).

Jesus said, "You have seen me, you have seen the Father" (John 14:9). This goes beyond incarnational theology.

Jesus said, "If you will not believe what I say, at least believe the things that I do" (John 10:38).

To receive favor from God, be more like Him. To be more like God, deepen your relationship with Him. To have that deeper relationship with God, you must know God's ways more. Growing like God helps us do God's work. When we do God's work, we gain favor with God.

People who spend a lot of time together share similar values. They walk alike, talk alike, and reason alike. That's why they like each other so much.

If you truly want God to like you—show you his favor, spend more time with God so you can be like God.

Want More for God's People

> Consider, too, that this nation is your
> people.

While talking to God, Moses requested to know his ways and reminded him that the nation was his people. Moses called them God's people. Moses encouraged God to consider that the nation Moses was leading was God's people. The nation belonged to God.

Moses' expressed his request like this. "Do these things for me if I am who you say I am. Don't forget, I'm leading your people as well. God, because I am leading your people, it is in your best interest, and the interest of your people, that you show me your ways so that I can know you better and gain more favor in your sight."

Now that's challenging. Not how we think we should talk when talking with God, but this is how Moses talked with God.

Your relationship has a direct bearing on the relationship God's people have with God. The weaker a pastor's relationship with God, the weaker his leadership will be. The weaker his leadership, the greater the impact it will have on the church's relationship with God. Sheep depend on the shepherd for direction. If the shepherd wanders, so do the sheep.

While I have placed great emphasis on your relationship with God, your role as pastor directly affects your people. Perhaps God calls those who, even to their turmoil, love others so deeply that it is hard to disconnect themselves from them. Because Moses cares for his people, he, as leader, seeks a deeper relationship for the sake of his people.

As pastors, we understand, our spiritual well-being influences those we are called to lead. While we pray for ourselves, it's not just ourselves we are thinking of. We are thinking of those God has sent us to lead.

So yes, show us your ways Lord so that we can know you, so we can gain more favor in your eyes, but also Lord, because you have called us to lead your people. Think of your people, Lord.

5

PRESENCE AND REST

God said, "My presence will go with you, and
I will give you rest."

Exodus 33:14

As GOD TOLD MOSES, God promises to be with us. He
promises we, too, will find rest.

God's Presence

My presence will go with you...

In the prayer of Moses of Exodus 33, God promises Moses he would go with him. God promised to go with Moses, despite Moses' uncertainty about who would accompany him. Moses had already witnessed God's presence in the cloud and fire, accompanied by a guiding and protective angel. To readers of the Exodus story, God's presence was obvious. Moses, however, seemed to miss it. He missed it much like we do when we are struggling.

Often, even though we too know the promises of God and may have even witnessed the incredible power of God, we still feel alone. We may even question why God has abandoned us. God hasn't, of course. It just feels that way.

Jesus taught, "Those who love me will keep my word, and my Father will love them, and we will come to them and make our home with them"(John 14:23).

Elsewhere, Jesus taught, "If you love me, you will keep my commandments. And I will ask the Father, and he will give you another Advocate, to be with you forever" (John 14:15).

In what we call The Great Commission, Jesus promised to be with always until the end of time (Matthew 28:16-20).

God promises his presence to us as his child. God, Jesus, and the Holy Spirit are with us. We are not alone.

God's Rest

...I will give you rest.

When we face Resignation Monday, we are exhausted. We are tired. We feel frustrated and anxious. Angst runs through our veins. Resignation Monday can be one of the most wearisome days of our lives, especially if it occurs often.

We experience God's rest by following his ways.

Jeremiah wrote: "Thus says the Lord: Stand at the crossroads and look, and ask for the ancient paths, where the good way lies; and walk in it, and find rest for your souls" (Jeremiah 6:16).

Jeremiah doesn't say, prop up against a rock or under a shade tree and you will find rest. Jeremiah says walk in the good way. We find rest by walking in the ways of God.

Isaiah declared: "Have you not known? Have you not heard? The Lord is the everlasting God, the Creator of the ends of the earth. He does not faint or grow weary; his understanding is unsearchable. He gives power to the faint and strengthens the powerless. Even youths will faint and be weary, and the young will fall exhausted, but those who wait for the Lord shall renew their strength; they shall mount up with wings like eagles; they shall run and not be weary; they shall walk and not faint" (Isaiah 40:28-31).

Isaiah taught the rest we seek comes from running and walking. We run and walk because God strengthens us. God strengthens us through our obedience to him.

Jesus said, "Come to me, all who labor and are heavy laden, and I will give you rest. Take my yoke upon you, and learn from me, for I am gentle and lowly in heart, and you will find rest for your souls. For my yoke is easy, and my burden is light" (Matthew 11:18-20).

Belief in Jesus prevents inner turmoil. Jesus even says the rest he gives comes from taking his yoke upon us. Yoking an ox is for field work, not napping in the barn. Gods' rest comes from doing the work of God.

Let's remember something of critical importance about the promise of rest. God is not saying for us to kick off our shoes, lay back in our recliners under a plush comforter, with our head resting on a down pillow. The rest God promises comes from trusting in him and following his teachings.

When we labor and toil in anxiety and stress, not in the ways of God, we become tired and weary. Such turmoil drives us to crying out, "I'm exhausted." We are exhausted!

We are exhausted because we seek peace in our church, how well it is doing, whether our people like us, or if we all get along.

Jesus proclaimed, "Peace I leave with you; my peace I give to you. I do not give to you as the world gives. Do not let your hearts be troubled, and do not let them be afraid" (John 14:27).

The peace—the rest—that God gives is found in the ways of God.

6

WANT GOD WITH YOU

And he said to him, "If your presence will not
go, do not bring us up from here. For how
shall it be known that I have found favor in
your sight, I and your people, unless you go
with us? In this way, we shall be distinct, I and
your people, from every people on the face of
the earth."

Exodus 33:15-16

UP TO THIS POINT in our reflection, the primary focus has
been upon ourselves. Our reflection has been about our

relationship with God. We have looked at our calling, both as Christian and pastor. We've seen God is with us, both as Christian and pastor. God knows us by name, and we have found favor with God, assuming we have been faithful to God. We seek to know God more by understanding his ways, which will enhance the favor we already have. We've also acknowledged, even calling God to acknowledge, that the people we lead aren't our people, they are God's people. Thus, as a leader called by God, our relationship with him has a direct bearing upon his people.

Yet, we are not selfish. As much as we understand the importance of our relationship with God, we think of our people. Because of knowing the joy of walking with the Lord, we want our people to walk with the Lord.

Wanting God to Go

> If your presence will not go, do not bring us
> up from here.

Without God's presence, everything we do is futile. The Psalmist even says, "Unless the Lord builds the house, those who build it labor in vain. Unless the Lord guards the city, the guard keeps watch in vain" (Psalm 127:1).

It's a reminder that without God, our work is nothing other than toil.

Moses understood this principle. He understood unless God went with them, it wouldn't matter. "If you are not going with us, leave us right where we are."

Moses made a strong ultimatum, and it made his point well. However, the reality is we can still pastor, even without God. It may be just a job, but we can still pastor.

We can lead a church like a CEO. We can continue the plans, programs, budgets, and even worship, with or without God. As Eugene Peterson[1] wrote:

> "...pastors are abandoning their posts, left and right, and at an alarming rate...Their names remain of the church stationary, and they continue to appear in pulpits on Sundays. But they are abandoning their posts, their calling...pastors.... have metamorphosed into a company of shopkeepers, and the shops they

---

1. Peterson, Eugene. Working the Angles: The Shave of Pastoral Integrity. Grand Rapids: Eerdmans, 1987.

keep are churches. They are preoccupied with the shopkeeper's concerns—how to keep the customer happy, how to lure customers away from competitors down the street, how to package the goods so that the customers will lay out more money."

Eugene Peterson, Working the Angles

Yes, absurd as it sounds, we can continue to do ministry without God. By doing so, we exclude God. Most likely we will find ourselves exhausted, frustrated, and tired; even defeated by Satan and sin. I suspect that going without God is a guarantee Resignation Monday is going to occur often.

This isn't what we want, though. We are not looking for a career. We want God to go with us. A constant topic of conversation we should have includes asking God to go with us. We should express that if he doesn't, the futility of our present circumstances will remain.

We ask God to go with us so we won't be just another shopkeeper—a business, an organization.

Wanting Others to Know

For how shall it be known that I have found
favor in your sight, I and your people,
unless you go with us?

God's presence is an indicator that we have found favor with God. The Bible's ancient stories, including Exodus, demonstrated to nations that God stood with Israel. It was clear. They could see it.

When God is with us, it is noticeable. God's spirit is clear in a pastor. It is noticeable in your church as well. We cannot hide our church's radiance when God's presence is with us. It's like a shining city on a hill. It will shine. Joy and happiness will flow like rivers from faithful followers of Jesus. Jesus said, "Out of the believer's heart shall flow rivers of living water" (John 7:38). This image of the people of God is too powerful to hide.

God is the foundation of our identity as a Christian, pastor, and church. Without God, we lose that identity. We are God's chosen people. We are the people of the promise.

Everything ties us to God. God must be present or our claim about God is questionable.

We can claim the favor of God all we want. We can buy a T-shirt, license plate, or bumper sticker declaring God favors us. We can stand before crowds and announce it, but without God, we are but a banging gong. Our words are meaningless.

Our request is that God goes with us, and our people, so others will know we are who we say we are, and God favors us. God makes us different.

Wanting to be Distinct

> In this way, we shall be distinct, I and your people, from every people on the face of the earth.

The second reason we ask for God to go with us is that God's presence makes us different from the rest of the world. God's presence gives us the power and strength to overcome sin, evil, and the wicked forces of this world. We cannot do this on our own. The prophet Zechariah declared, "Not by might, not by power, but by the spirit of the Lord" (Zechariah 4:6).

This ability to overcome evil creates us into peculiar people. We become people that love one another. We have joy, peace, patience, and kindness. Generosity, faithfulness, gentleness, and self-control describe us. These attributes set us apart from everyone else.

A central part of our message is that Christ makes us different. The first post-Easter message preached urged people to leave a corrupt generation and act as God's people, not the world (Acts 2:40).

Isn't this what we desire on Resignation Monday? Isn't this what we seek? Our aim is to experience God's presence so vividly that we can feel it, sense it, and recognize it. We want everyone to know it—our people and others.

It is God's presence that makes us distinct, and unlike the world. It is what sets us apart and even provides an example that draws others to God.

7

BECAUSE OF YOU

The Lord said to Moses, "I will also do this
thing that you have asked, for you have found
favor in my sight, and I know you by name."

Exodus 33:17

CAN ONE MAN'S PRAYER matter?

When we study the story of Exodus, we discover the
people never prayed God would go with them. They didn't
pray for favor or to know God's ways or anything else. Only
Moses prayed for these things. You are the one who must
pray.

If you experience Resignation Monday, frustration with the church may be the source. Their lack of interest in God may cause you anger. You must still fulfill your pastoral role. God is the only one who can release you from your responsibility. Unless God released you, most likely you are just frustrated.

Your prayer can matter. You, and you alone, can change the course of everything, even if you are the only one affected.

"And I sought for anyone among them who would repair the wall and stand in the breach before me on behalf of the land, so that I would not destroy it, but I found no one" (Ezekiel 22:30).

You stand in the breach. God looks for someone like you. You act like God when you pray for others. You are interceding like the Holy Spirit. Some may even say you are interceding like Jesus. As we have learned, when you live your life in the ways of God, you find favor with God.

God granted Moses' request, including going with the people. God granted that request because Moses found favor before God and God knew his name. Moses was the reason. It was his intercession that made the difference.

While we don't enjoy placing such great emphasis upon ourselves, our relationship with Jesus may determine if God goes with our church.

Yours Already

The irony of our requests is God has already promised what we ask for. It's like God has said to us, you can have this anytime you want it. It's yours already. Claim it. Simply receive it.

Despite God telling us it's ours, we still ask for it as if it isn't. We ask as if God never promised it or as if we're clueless about how to get it.

God tells us how to have what we seek. We must follow his instructions to get it. And what he calls us to do isn't out of our reach. It's not too hard for us. We just need to do what God does.

Let's consider what he have asked for so far in this book. We have asked for God to show us his ways. God has done that already. We have the Word of God that tells us that. Jesus taught if we have seen him; we have seen the father. He also taught us how to live our lives. We have the Holy Spirit, who teaches us as well. One could say we have the story of the ancient church showing disciples living out the ways of God. So, we know the ways of God.

We have asked God to consider his people. There is a connection between our relationship as pastor and God considering those called by his name. Yet, without doubt, God knows his people. He remembers them. Scriptures reveal God remembered the Israelites as he promised and as his people. We have no reason to think God has forgotten his people. It's not like he ever forgets, and we needed to ask him to think hard and focus on recalling those called by his name. He hasn't become distracted that he forgot about something. God remembers. We already have what we asked for.

We requested God's presence. Be with us. God has always been with his people. God was with Moses. He filled the tabernacle in their midst. God filled the temple. He sent his son, Jesus, who was also called Emmanuel—God with us. Mary, Elizabeth, Simeon, and a host of others declared the same thing. Jesus taught us he was with us. Jesus promised to send the Holy Spirit, which he did and still does. He promised to be with us as we fulfilled the great commission. The Book of Acts revealed God amid the ancient church. So yes, God with us. We have that too.

Ironically, we have everything we seek. God has promised it. God has given it. All that we ask is ours already.

Recall the story of the Prodigal Son, as it is often called. The father comforted the older son by telling him that all he had belonged to him (Luke 15:31). Everything God promised is already ours. We must acknowledge it, accept it, and then get on with the celebration.

But let's not forget, there are conditions to remember. God expects something from us if we are to know and have God's presence. We must be obedient. We must be like God by following the ways of God.

There is no knowing God without taking the time to learn God's ways. Only by following God's ways can we gain his favor. Without living by God's ways, we can't expect his presence. We can't expect to be known as favored if we are disobedient. We can't be distinct if we look like the world. To distinguish ourselves, we must live according to the Kingdom of God rather than the world.

Like the oldest brother in the story of the prodigal son, what God promises is ours already. We must live like it is ours. The problem is, like the oldest brother, we haven't been living it. Sometimes, it's our people that haven't been living it. At other times, it is us that haven't been faithful.

If we want to experience God's presence and ways to the extent they grow our relationship with Him, give us more favor, and make us distinct, we must be obedient.

8

NOTHING, NOT EVEN THE CHURCH

"For I am convinced that neither death, nor
life, nor angels, nor rulers, nor things present,
nor things to come, nor powers, nor height,
nor depth, nor anything else in all creation
will be able to separate us from the love of
God in Christ Jesus our Lord."

Romans 8:38-39

IF WE ARE OBEDIENT, nothing can sever our relationship
with God. What our church does or doesn't do can't

change our walk with God. I think what the Apostle Paul teaches applies to this situation.

Often, we apply those verses to external powers, as in evil and wickedness. We say the enemy can't ever separate us from God.

Our friends, our allies, or the church can separate either. The internal conflicts that arise within the body of Christ can't separate us from the love of the Lord.

The Apostle Paul's letters to the churches, except for one, involved correcting something or someone in the church. Paul addressed problems, debates, and arguments. Sometimes they were major doctrinal debates. Sometimes it was little things like waiting for everyone to arrive before eating.

If we had to endure what Paul did, we would have resigned earlier. Some of Paul's frustrations came from outside the church. Most came from within the Christian community.

Proverbs 14:4 states where there is no ox, the barn will be clean.

If you want a clean barn, get rid of the ox.

Church-goers bring problems. People come with issues. It's all part of having people in your church.

The only solution for a mess-free church is to eliminate people. Your church will not have any issues. It will also lack people.

Proverbs 14:4 continues by telling us, "The strength of an ox produces much."

Since we don't refer to ourselves as oxen in the church, rather we use the term sheep, a potential paraphrase of Proverbs 14:4 might be: "A clean church lacks sheep, but the strength of sheep produces much."

Consider how much good the church produces. Consider everything that takes place, from worship, to Sunday School, to vacation bible school. Some churches have feeding programs. Some take part in global giving programs through their denomination. Churches excel at praying for others. Churches produce great good for the Kingdom of God.

Again, don't think God has sent you to perfect people. God has sent you to an imperfect people so you can lead them. If they were perfect, they wouldn't need leading. They would lead themselves.

The problem isn't with your people. Your people are doing what people do. Yes, it can get messy. But your people also produce a lot of good.

This brings us back to that recurring principle we have mentioned in this book. The key to it all is your relationship with the Lord. Your church, and the frustrations of the church, can't separate you from the love of the Lord. Your relationship with Christ makes you Christian and the reason God called you into ministry. The key is discovering how your relationship can get you through Resignation Monday and back to effective congregational leadership.

PRECISION FAITH RECAP

LET'S DO A RECAP. I know we keep rehashing things, but since the prayer of Moses involves remembering, it is important to remind ourselves. Use this list as thoughts for reflection as you pray.

1. You are experiencing Resignation Monday. Lots of us have been there. It's real.

2. You know what to do first. Run to your place of meeting. You're going where you feel closest to God.

3. You go to your place of God because you know the first person you need to talk to is God.

4. There, you remember you are a child of God. No

matter what happens, what you decide, God loves you. He loved you way before you became a pastor.

5. You remember also that God is the one who called you to pastor. He called you before he ever sent you to anyone. What he called you to do has nothing to do with how others respond. It's your calling, not theirs.

6. He called you into ministry and promised to be with you throughout. The promise is more relevant to being a follower than a pastor. God sent no one to do his work alone.

7. You remember God knows you by name.

8. God favors you, assuming you have been obedient.

9. You have asked to know God's ways, even though God has already shown you that.

10. You want to know God's ways so that you can know him more. It is all about your relationship with him.

11. Because of knowing God's ways and knowing God more, you can gain more favor from God. How?

By integrating what you have learned about God into your life.

12. You are not ignorant of the fact that your relationship with God has a direct bearing on God's people you lead. They are his. They are not yours.

13. You want God's presence for you and your people. Again, God has already given this. You, or your people, may not be aware of it. But God is there.

14. You know it is God's presence that will set you apart as favored, and as distinct. Again, this only works if you follow God's ways.

15. You have also taken a moment to remind yourself, people bring problems. People also bring positive results. Without them, there is no church. You must have them.

9

Want God's Glory

Moses said, "Please show me your glory."

Exodus 33:18

Glory is an interesting word in the Bible. The Bible speaks of God's glory as the physical presence of God. It refers to the acts of God. Those who could see it even described God's glory.

> "In Christ we have also obtained an inheritance, having been destined according to the purpose of him who accomplishes all

things according to his counsel and will, so that we, who were the first to set our hope on Christ, might live for the praise of his glory."

Ephesians 1:11-12

"I will say to the north, 'Give them up,' and to the south, 'Do not withhold; bring my sons from far away and my daughters from the end of the earth—everyone who is called by my name, whom I created for my glory, whom I formed and made.'"

Isaiah 43:6-7

"For as the loincloth clings to one's loins, so I made the whole house of Israel and the whole house of Judah cling to me, says the Lord, in order that they might be for me a people, a name, a praise, and a glory."

Jeremiah 13:11

"I will harden Pharaoh's heart, and he will pursue them, so that I will gain glory for myself over Pharaoh and all his army, and the Egyptians shall know that I am the Lord." And they did so.

Exodus 14:4

"In the same way, let your light shine before others, so that they may see your good works and give glory to your Father in heaven."

Matthew 5:16

"And as Aaron spoke to the whole congregation of the Israelites, they looked toward the wilderness, and the glory of the Lord appeared in the cloud."

Exodus 16:10

"Then the cloud covered the tent of meeting, and the glory of the Lord filled the tabernacle."

Exodus 40:34

Other Bible passages speak of the Lord's glory. They all reveal the same pattern and trend. God's glory is something God can gain and something the people give to God. God already possesses glory. God's glory describes his presence. Glory is something God reveals and something resulting from God's actions.

So, what are we asking for when we request to see God's glory?

While we can't say what Moses was asking to see, we get the idea he was asking to see God himself. Moses either sought proof or desired to be in God's presence.

What are we seeking when we to ask to see God's glory?

Perhaps we could nail it down to one specific thing. Most likely, we are asking for several things.

As described in the verses already referenced, what we are seeking is God himself in all the manifestations of his glory. We seek God's very presence. We hope to witness his strength and power. We seek for God to be glorified by our people. God's Holy Spirit, like a rushing wind, is something we welcome.

Our hope is in God on Resignation Monday. I'm not sure we care how God acts, just that he does.

In our minds, seeing God's glory would prevent us from quitting. If God showed up, our problems would disappear. Our people would give God more glory if he showed his glory. They would quit fighting with one another. Our people would trust our leadership. They would start obeying.

Should that be our focus? Should our focus be to see God's glory so our people will behave?

The Bible shows even with God amid the people; they rebelled against God. Even with God among them, historically, God's people struggle.

If our hope is in how other people respond with God's presence, we may be in trouble. So why ask for God's glory?

You are asking for God's glory for yourself. You are asking to see it for yourself. The transformation and change that you hope God's glory brings starts with you. Perhaps you need God's glory to rekindle your calling, to give you hope, maybe even power and strength. Nothing wrong with any of those desires. You should desire them always. That's why you ask for God's glory.

When Moses asked for it, he didn't have the people in mind. This was a one-on-one personal revelation Moses was seeking. By experiencing God's glory, Moses led the people into following God, and they saw God's glory, but Moses started with himself.

10

CONDITIONS

I will do whatever you ask in my name, so that
the Father may be glorified in the Son. If in my
name you ask me for anything, I will do it.

John 14:13-14

IN MOST CASES, EVEN though God may grant what we ask for, there are conditions. God granted Moses' request to see God's glory, but there were conditions.

First, a protective condition guarded Moses. God told Moses no one could see his face and live (Exodus 33:19). Sometimes there are limits to what God grants us. We may not get everything we ask for because God knows it is not good for us. God may open a different door than the one we requested. If God opened that door, it would not be beneficial for us. Some of God's conditions protect us.

Second, there are conditions for what we must do. God told Moses what he was to do before he could see his glory (Exodus 33:21-23). Moses must come ready to take notes. He must come ready to receive. Moses must go exactly where he says and do exactly what he is told.

Likewise, God tells us what we must do to see his glory. Jesus taught that there are conditions for having God and Christ within oneself. Jesus said we must love and obey him (John 14:15-21). We are not different than Moses. If we are to experience God's glory we must come ready to learn and to receive. We must do exactly what God says and do exactly what we are told.

Through the Old Testament prophets, God proclaimed to Israel that they had to change the way they lived. Change was necessary for them to know God's presence. It was required for God to heal their land. God made statements with if-then implications. This action produces this result. No action, no result.

While we protestants often proclaim God's grace as the unmerited, undeserving love of God, we are not talking about God's love here. Without question, the scriptures reveal God's grace. However, this does not mean we can disobey God without consequences.

Again, there are no conditions for God's love. God loves us. He loves us even while we are sinners. His love for us is why he sent his son. However, there are conditions to the abundant life that Jesus promises. For us to live the abundant life promised, we must love and keep the teachings and commands of God. We cannot circumvent this truth as much as we may want to.

We walk this fine line of being God's people and living as God's people. The Bible reminds us of expectations for Christian discipleship. The Gospels reinforce Jesus expects something. Jesus has conditions.

You cannot expect to live a Spirit-filled life while pursuing the works of the flesh. The Apostle John even taught you cannot say you know Jesus if you do not obey Jesus. John has a name for you if you think you can. He used the word liar. On the other hand, if you abide in Jesus, you will walk just as he walked (1 John 2).

Conditions. There are conditions. If we want to see the glory of God, God tells us how.

God desires to show us his glory. God longs to reveal himself. God wants to declare his name and his ways.

"And without faith it is impossible to please him, for whoever would approach God must believe that he exists and that he rewards those who seek him" (Hebrews 11:6).

> "But seek first the kingdom of God and his righteousness, and all these things will be given to you as well."
>
> Matthew 6:33

> "Ask, and it will be given to you; search, and you will find; knock, and the door will be opened for you."
>
> Matthew 7:7

> "When you search for me, you will find me; if you seek me with all your heart."
>
> Jeremiah 29:13

> "Seek the Lord while he may be found; call upon him while he is near."

Isaiah 55:6

"From there you will seek the Lord your God,
and you will find him if you search after him
with all your heart and soul."

Deuteronomy 4:29

"I love those who love me, and those who seek
me diligently find me."

Proverbs 8:17

Even the Psalmist understood the seeking God implied
not wandering from the commandments of God.

"With my whole heart I seek you; do not let
me stray from your commandments."

Psalm 119:10

If we ask to see God's glory, we must be prepared to
do what God says to experience it. As Dick Wills points

out in Waking to God's Dream, God blesses obedience. [1] God does not bless disobedience. The greatest blessing isn't anything external. The greatest blessing is God himself, knowing and experiencing God's glory in our lives.

Your relationship with God is what matters. Relying on others' experience of God is risky and dangerous. We may not always see others share our relationship with God. Not even Jesus had that experience. Yet, his joy remained. Jesus' joy wasn't based on whether his disciples, the people he taught, the religious leaders, or anyone else got it. Jesus' joy remained because of his relationship he had with his father.

---

1. Dick Wills. Waking to God's Dream: Spiritual Leadership and Church Renewal (Nashville: Abingdon, 1999) 33.

11

GOD'S WAYS

The Lord descended in the cloud and
stood with him there and proclaimed the
name, "The Lord." The Lord passed before
him and proclaimed, "The Lord, the Lord,
a God merciful and gracious, slow to
anger, and abounding in steadfast love and
faithfulness, keeping steadfast love for the
thousandth generation, forgiving iniquity
and transgression and sin, yet by no means
clearing the guilty, but visiting the iniquity
of the parents upon the children and the

children's children to the third and the
fourth generation."

Exodus 34:5-7

WHEN MOSES ASKED TO see God's glory, God granted his request with conditions. Moses followed God's conditions. As a result, Moses saw the glory of the Lord as promised. He also heard God proclaimed his ways to him.

Merciful

The Lord, the Lord, a God merciful...

God is merciful.

Traditional definitions define mercy as compassion or forbearance shown to an offender or one under another's power. Compassion isn't a feeling. Compassion is an act. It is how we treat another person, particularly those in distress.

Forbearance is a very interesting word. Forbearance means to refrain from enforcement of something that is due.

Right away, we find God is merciful. God shows compassion. He treats us with compassion. Not only that, but God also refrains from enforcing what is due him. God refrains from punishing people.

The author of Lamentations declares the reason God did not consume Israel was because of his mercy and compassion. The prophet proclaims that God's mercy and compassion renews every morning (Lamentations 3:22-23).

Jonah was mad at God for forgiving Israel's enemies rather than destroying them. Jonah knew God was merciful and eager not to punish people (Jonah 4:2).

God even forgave the evil King Manasseh because he prayed for God's mercy (2 Chronicles 33:12-13).

Let's keep in mind why we wanted God to show us his ways. We want to know God's ways so that we can know God more. By knowing God more, we discover how we are to act. By modeling our lives after God, we find more favor.

What's God's first way? God is merciful. Now, for us, sitting at our desks, ready to quit, we must ask ourselves, are we being merciful? Are we following God's ways?

If we are thinking about quitting, we are likely mad or hurt. Is our turning in the resignation letter an act of compassion for God's people? Are we in a roundabout way, enforcing something we think is due to us? After all, don't we deserve better? Right? Our people should treat us better.

What if God handed in a resignation letter because of our failures? Or what if God demanded punishment for when we rebelled against him?

We all know the answers to those hypothetical questions. But God did not do that. The gospel's message is that God, being compassionate, spared us from punishment by having Christ take it for us. Not only that, but Jesus also taught us to be merciful.

"Be merciful, just as your Father is merciful" (Luke 6:36).

Jesus tells us that by being merciful, we receive mercy (Matthew 5:7).

James warns that judgement awaits for those who are not merciful (James 2:13).

If we are going to proclaim God's ways, and follow God's ways, then we can't have a different standard than God. We must live and act like God. Just as God hasn't given up on us, we can't give up on our people.

Gracious

The Lord, the Lord, a God... gracious...

God is gracious.

We define gracious as kindness and courtesy.

Grace is the root word of gracious. We define grace as God's unmerited and undeserving love. God is kind to us. God is courteous to us. He is not harsh. He is not rude. Condescending wouldn't be a term to describe God as gracious. Rather, God loves us even though we don't deserve it. God cares for us, even though our actions do not merit such love.

The Bible shows God longs to be gracious. He looks for opportunities to give grace.

There are over 330 instances of God's graciousness in the Bible. God's grace is mentioned in the Law, the Prophets, the Poetry and Wisdom writings, Gospels, and the Epistles. God's grace appears in every section of the Bible.

> "Therefore the Lord waits to be gracious to you."
>
> Isaiah 30:18

It's interesting how we who stand in the gap for God often forget God expects us to be like him. How many times do we hold our people to measure up? How often do we withhold love, kindness, and courtesy because we feel they don't deserve it?

Pastoral leadership is both ironic and difficult. God calls us to lead as he shows us how to lead. How he shows us to lead is hard and difficult. He calls us to love our people, regardless. He asks us to show them God's grace even when their actions do not merit such love.

Slow to Anger

The Lord, the Lord, a God... slow to anger...

God is slow to anger.

We've said this already. Many times, when we are considering resigning, we are angry. We are angry at someone. Something that someone said set us off. The mere fact complacency was on every face in the congregations, upsets us. Sometimes we are angry that our church isn't where we thought it would be now. We are angry that we aren't where we thought we would be in our careers. We are angry because the leadership board did not approve something. Anger leads us to the drawer where we keep the letter.

Sometimes getting angry is necessary. Anger can move us to action. The Bible cautions us that while we may get angry, we must not sin.

The Psalmist said, "When you are disturbed, do not sin; ponder it on your beds, and be silent" (Psalm 4:4). In other words, don't act on your anger. Rather, as the Psalmist continues in the next verse, we should worship and trust the Lord (4:5).

The Apostle Paul wrote the same thing to the Ephesians, teaching them to not let the sun go down on their anger (Ephesians 4:26). Paul connects, holding anger as making room for the devil.

God being slow to anger makes us ask, "Am I resigning out of anger?" "Am I acting on my anger?" "Is my actions resulting from anger, sinning?" "Have I made room for the devil in my anger and is what I am about to do listening to Satan rather than God?"

Perhaps the best course of action is to not resign when we are angry. Maybe we should wait until the anger subsides? Once we have control over our anger, and we are sure that resigning is the right decision, we can submit our letter.

Another aspect surrounding anger is to ask, "Is what I am experiencing right now a response to quick anger? Is where

I find myself a hasty reaction? Did something set me off and now I am pondering moving on?"

Maybe it has been a slow, drawn-out anger. Maybe you have, over time, striving to be patient, merciful, and kind reached your limit. We need to consider how God is slow to anger and not let our anger, particularly hasty anger, lead us to do something drastic.

Let's not forget, it was Moses' anger that kept him from entering the Promised Land. Jesus also taught us not to be angry with others. In fact, if we held that anger without addressing it, we were in danger of judgment (Matthew 5:22-25).

Basing our Resignation Monday decision on anger is not wise. Slowing that anger, following the example of God, is wise.

Abundance of Steadfast Love

The Lord, the Lord, a God... abounding in steadfast love...

God shows an abundance of steadfast love.

We define steadfast as fixed and not subject to change. We connect steadfast with deep loyalty.

According to God's announcement regarding his actions, not only does he have steadfast love, but he also has an abundance of steadfast love. His love never changes, and he will always remain loyal.

I would hope that your love for your people never changes. You love them regardless of their response to you and your leadership. Make no mistake, pastors like to be loved as well. It feels good when our people get behind us and follow our leadership. Our love for them, however, cannot be based on their love for us. We love our people because they are God's people. We love our people because God loves them.

Paul reminds us that even while we were yet sinners, God proves his love for us. Christ died for us even though we remained in our sins (Romans 5:8). God didn't wait for us to get it right for him to show his love. Some might say, because we couldn't get it right, God loved us.

Recall the first attribute of God—compassion. Compassion is an act toward those in distress. Nothing is more distressing than being in sin. Yet, in our sin, God has compassion upon us. God loves us.

Can you love your people even when they are yet sinners? Can you follow God's example?

Let us remember, because of God's love, Christ suffered. Loving isn't easy. We associate love and loving with feel-good emotions. Joy, happiness, and warmth come to mind. However, love produces suffering. We suffer because we love. We endure because we love.

The Apostle Paul wrote the following about love: "Love is patient; love is kind; love is not envious or boastful or arrogant or rude. It does not insist on its own way; it is not irritable; it keeps no record of wrongs; it does not rejoice in wrongdoing but rejoices in the truth. It bears all things, believes all things, hopes all things, endures all things. Love never ends" (1 Corinthians 13:4-8).

Can you endure whatever has put you in the resignation debate? Can you be patient with your people, being kind in the process? Can you not insist it is your way, or the highway? Can you refrain from keeping a record of your people disappointing you? Can you show an abundance of steadfast love?

Abundance of Steadfast Faithfulness

> The Lord, the Lord, a God... abounding in
> steadfast... faithfulness...

God shows an abundance of steadfast faithfulness.

God fixes his faithfulness, just like his love, without limits. God is committed.

God committed to his people from the beginning. He promised to never abandon them. Now, there were consequences for the times Israel was disobedient, but God remained faithful. God also told the Israelites what they needed to do to have their land restored and to prosper. Throughout the Israelite story, there were times they responded to God's call and there were times they did not. Yet God was always present. God never gave up. God kept trying.

God shows us his ways so we can follow them. Moses wanted to know God's ways so he would know how to lead. The Psalmist also made such a request.

"Make me to know your ways, O Lord;
teach me your paths. Lead me in your truth
and teach me, for you are the God of my
salvation; for you I wait all day long."

Psalm 25:4-5

The Psalmist sought God's ways to walk the right paths. He wanted the Lord to lead him so he would know where to walk. All to say, show me so I can walk not only with you, but like you.

In this period of discernment, look to God. Be faithful as God is faithful. Can you keep trying? Can you not give up? Calling your people to follow God, can you remain faithful?

One Who Keeps Steadfast Love for Generations

The Lord, the Lord, a God... keeping steadfast love for the thousandth generation...

God's love extends beyond those present.

The best way to explain this love is to imagine what it looks like in practice. Go back to the Exodus story. Imagine all the people Moses led out of Egypt. They stand at the mountain's base, looking up at the cloud of God's presence. God is beholding them from the cloud of smoke. God loves them. It is for this reason, God delivered them. Yet God doesn't just love those gathered. God loves their children not yet born. God's hope isn't just for those assembled. His hope is for their offspring, and their offspring's offspring. When God loves, his love extends to generations not yet born—to future generations.

Recall the prayer of Jesus recorded in John 17. Jesus didn't limit his prayer to his disciples. Jesus prayed even for those not yet. He prayed for those who would believe through his disciples (John 17:20).

This presents an amazing transition in the way we love as pastors. To emulate God, our love must mirror God's ways. We don't just love the people that are gathered on the current Sunday. We love those not yet. We love their children, and even their children's children. Following Jesus' example, we love those who will one day worship with us because of those present today.

Imagine leading your congregation with the future in mind. Certainly, you hope your present congregation is part of the future, but many of them will not be. Some will have passed to be with the Lord. Others will move for employment and family reasons. A few may leave your church or the church all together. But the love that flows from your pastoral leadership extends not to your present congregation alone, but also to the generations that follow.

That's a novel and profound approach to ministry. Imagine saying to your people, "I intend not just to love you, but your descendants. I intend to be the pastor of this church for future generations."

In some denominations, this isn't practical. Some denominations appoint pastors and move them as needed to meet the overall mission of the church. Yet, this does not prevent us from having this mindset in ministry. We love our people, even though the church may move us someday.

Forgiving

The Lord, the Lord, a God... forgiving iniquity, transgression, and sin...

God is forgiving.

We define forgiveness as allowing room for error or weakness. If we applied this definition to God, then we are saying God allows room for error and weakness.

What is more amazing, however, is that God applies this description of himself to three areas—iniquity, transgression, and sin. We sometimes consider these three areas as the same. They are not identical; they are distinct.

Iniquity

> The Lord, the Lord, a God... forgiving iniquity...

God forgives iniquity.

God forgiving iniquity is often hard to accept. Yet, God declares he forgives iniquity.

We consider iniquity, of all offenses, the worst. Iniquity is a gross injustice or a gross, wicked act. The adjective gross isn't because sin is gruesome. We use that term because someone thought out and planned wickedness. We are not talking about slipping up or an abrupt reaction. To use a Biblical pattern, iniquity is when one lies on their bed plotting and planning the action. Those who scheme to trap others are guilty of iniquity. We could say that those who premeditate actions on their bed are committing iniquity. A person goes into a situation planning to commit a sin, knowing full well it is a sin.

The prophet Micah provides a good definition:

> "Woe to those who devise wickedness and
> evil deeds on their beds! When the morning
> dawns, they perform it, because it is in their
> power."
>
> Micah 2:1

That's iniquity. You get the picture.

Guess what? God forgives iniquity. That is hard for us to swallow. We want justice, extreme justice in such cases. In fact, in matters of law, the punishment is greater for such crimes. Yet, according to God's description of himself, he forgives this type of sin.

I learned about a church where a group undermined the leadership of the pastor. They created a plan and executed it. They met in groups with other church members to advocate their plan. They went to the homes of fellow church members. They held secret meetings. When it came to light, the pastor faced a decision. How was he going to respond? Could he forgive them? The pastor chose to forgive them. The church prospered, even though the group stayed. In fact, the leader of that group became a close friend and confident of the pastor. No one from the group asked for forgiveness, ironically. Not once did they apologize. Yet, the pastor forgave them.

Keep in mind that forgiveness rests with the offended. It is the offended that grants forgiveness. Forgiveness isn't based on the offender. An apology isn't required. I know that sounds counterintuitive, but it is true.

Recall Jesus and Stephen, as they were dying. They asked God to forgive those who persecuted them. Those who persecuted them didn't apologize for their actions. They may have never been sorry for their actions. Yet, Jesus, and Stephen, asked God to forgive them (Luke 23:34 and Acts 7:60).

Jesus once taught his disciples that they had the power to forgive sins (John 20:23).

God forgives iniquity, even the thought-out, pre-planned acts of sin. Can we, as pastors, act similarly, especially when angry and considering leaving because of others' actions?

Transgressions

> The Lord, the Lord, a God... forgiving...
> transgression...

God forgives transgressions.

Unlike iniquity, we knowingly commit transgressions, but without premeditated malice. People commit transgressions, but not with the same level of intent. We choose to transgress in the moment, despite knowing it disobeys God.

Transgression is like seeing a stop sign. You know you should stop. But because you don't feel like it, you drive right through it.

Transgression is to know the truth, but choose to lie instead.

Transgression could be when the church knows they should give to the poor, homeless, hungry, and orphans. They choose not to, however, because they would rather keep the money for themselves.

I cannot help but think of the Lord's Prayer. We pray, "Forgive us our transgressions, as we forgive those who transgress against us."

When our people are unwilling to follow the teachings of Jesus, we can indeed get frustrated to the extent of resigning. Can we forgive them and continue to lead them? Can we follow the ways of God and forgive their transgressions?

Sins

> The Lord, the Lord, a God... forgiving... sin...

God forgives sins.

While we may classify iniquity and transgressions as sin, sin is different. Some argue that sin is just sin. That would be true as well. But for understanding more about God's ways, let's look at sin differently from iniquity and transgressions. Iniquity and transgression are levels of sins. For our purpose, let's think of sin as an unintentional act of disobedience. Sin are those times we do something when we don't mean to. Knee-jerk reactions, if you will.

We didn't mean to snap at someone, we just did. Is it still a sin? Yes, indeed. But we didn't intentionally decide to snap at a person. We didn't lie on our bed contemplating how we could snap at someone. Is it still snapping? Yes, but it is different.

The reality is we make mistakes. We slip up. We don't intend to hurt others, but sometimes we do.

This happens in the church as much as it does anywhere else. Church squabbles often fall into this category. There isn't any premeditation involved. No one made a conscious decision to hurt someone. They spoke thoughtlessly, causing harm to others in the church. Some people lack a filter for their thoughts. They just blurt it out without ever considering others. Sometimes, people are so invested in their own ministry area that they cannot realize how their ministry affects other ministries. They are just passionate about what God has called them to do.

God forgives sin. As pastors, we must ask ourselves if we can forgive sin like God does? Can we be like God?

As we wrap this section up about forgiveness, let's mention a brief word here about forgiving others. Even though we forgive them, if they choose to continue their acts of transgressions, they can and will suffer. There are consequences of sin. Prophets pointed out that Israel suffered because of disobedience. God even declared that until they changed, they would continue to suffer, perhaps even worse.

So, as we talk about following the example of God's forgiveness, this does not mean everything will be easy. It will not be easy if our people continue to disobey God. Can we, as their pastor, however, continue to abide with them in hopes our obedience to God, our relationship with God, can guide them?

Holds Accountable

> The Lord, the Lord, a God... forgiving... yet
> by no means clearing the guilty...

God holds people accountable.

Up to this point, God has shown us his ways are all about mercy, grace, love, faithfulness, and forgiveness. Everything sounds super good to us. As pastors contemplating resigning, these attributes may sound super challenging. We may wish we had never heard them or reflected upon following the ways of God in our pastoral leadership.

That said, God isn't all mushy-gushy. God holds us accountable. In fact, the words he used to inform Moses of his accountability can raise questions for us.

"...yet by no means clearing the guilty, but visiting the iniquity of the parents upon the children and the children's children to the third and the fourth generation" (Exodus 34:7).

This passage has created much turmoil and angst among those who have reflected upon it. I have found many resources refused to deal with it at all. Maybe that is because of our broader understanding of God's accountability.

Ezekiel declared our children will not bear the guilt for the parent's sin, nor would the parent bear the guilt of the child's sin (Ezekiel 18:20).

The two passages appear contradictory. I am not trying to explain either away or even to reconcile them. However, the sins of the parents create consequences the children must deal with. Likewise, a child's sin can create consequences a parent must deal with.

God promises to forgive the sin, but that does not mean God undoes the consequences. Our sins, and the consequences, extend well beyond ourselves, our children, and children's children.

A person who has sinned in a way that produces consequences for her family has forced the rest of her family to live with her sin. Even if they choose to forgive her, and God forgives her, that choice has brought consequences that will forever be there.

A man who gambles his earnings away forces his family to live in poverty. Statistics show the odds are the family will continue in poverty unless an child can break free from it and bring the rest of the family with them.

I wonder if this is the message of God to us. He holds us accountable, particularly if we are unrepentant. He also holds us accountable by allowing the consequences of our actions to remain. Often, those consequences go beyond us and to the generations that follow.

Are those who suffer the consequences of our actions guilty? No. Yet the parent's actions create circumstances the children and children's children must live with. Likewise, when a child does something sinful, it creates far-reaching consequences. The parents, siblings, community, and perhaps even beyond, live with the consequences.

Paul taught creation itself groans for redemption (Romans 8:19). Strange to think that the sins of Adam and Eve, passed to us and our inclinations, affected all of creation. However, it did. The sinful action of humanity affects God's creation. God holds us accountable for destroying what he created for our good.

Sin's consequences have implications even upon creation itself. While God may forgive us, if we have lived with such consumption that our greed has damaged the earth, we must live with the results. The writer of Revelations even declares God punishes those who destroy the earth (Revelation 11:18).

When your people have committed sinful and hurtful acts, you may forgive them. However, the consequences of their actions may have a lasting impact.

After the Israelites refused to the enter the Promised Land, God remained their God, but they could not enter the Promised Land. Only their descendants were allowed to enter.

When Moses struck the rock in anger, God's punishment was Moses couldn't enter the Promised Land. Did God still love Moses? Yes. Did God forgive Moses? Apparently. According to the Gospels, Moses appeared with Elijah on the Mount of Transfiguration.

Yet still, the consequences of Moses' decision were lasting. The leaders witnessed his anger. God prohibited Moses from entering. Imagine how the people felt watching the man who had led them all this time not get to enter.

When we sin, there are consequences. Those consequences hold us accountable.

We must also hold our people accountable for their actions. While we may forgive them, we must correct them.

Paul instructing Timothy said,

> "In the presence of God and of Christ Jesus,
> who is to judge the living and the dead, and

in view of his appearing and his kingdom,
I solemnly urge you: proclaim the message;
be persistent whether the time is favorable or
unfavorable; convince, rebuke, and encourage
with the utmost patience in teaching."

2 Timothy 4:1-2

Paul told Titus to rebuke the rebellious among them so that may become of sound faith (Titus 1:13).

Writing to the Thessalonians, Paul said, "And we urge you, brothers and sisters, to admonish the idlers, encourage the fainthearted, help the weak, be patient with all of them" (1 Thessalonians 5:14).

Jesus taught: "If your brother or sister sins against you, go and point out the fault when the two of you are alone. If you are listened to, you have regained that one. But if you are not listened to, take one or two others along with you, so that every word may be confirmed by the evidence of two or three witnesses. If that person refuses to listen to them, tell it to the church, and if the offender refuses to listen even to the church, let such a one be to you as a gentile and a tax collector" (Matthew 18:15-17).

Jesus also taught, however, that if they were repentant, to forgive them.

"Be on your guard! If a brother or sister sins, you must rebuke the offender, and if there is repentance, you must forgive" (Luke 17:3).

We cannot neglect our pastoral role of accountability. Just because we follow the forgiving ways of God doesn't mean we shouldn't address their faults. We should address them; otherwise, we may disobey what we have learned from scripture.

PRECISION FAITH RECAP

WE HAVE COVERED A lot in such a little book. Let's do another quick recap.

1. It's Resignation Monday.

2. You know it is not a feeling you want, so you go to your special place of talking with God.

3. You remember you are a child of God.

4. You remember also that God called you.

5. God is with you. You are not alone.

6. God knows you by name.

7. God favors you.

8. You seek God's guidance amidst this turmoil.

9. You know by knowing God's ways, you will know God more and gain more favor in God's sight. After all, you have been seeking to please God.

10. You also know that your relationship with God affects God's people.

11. As part of your prayer, you may ask to know God's presence even more. You may even ask for God's presence with the people you lead.

12. You understand it is only God with you that will set you, and your people, apart.

13. The reality is leading people means you will face difficulties. It is inherit.

14. As you pray, you recall the ways of God.

   ◦ God is merciful.

   ◦ God is gracious.

   ◦ God is slow to anger.

   ◦ God has an abundance of steadfast love.

- God has an abundance of steadfast faithfulness.

- God keeps steadfast love for generations.

- God forgives iniquity.

- God forgives transgressions.

- God forgives sins.

- God holds accountable.

This book's intent is not for you not to resign. The purpose is to encourage you to reflect upon what you are experiencing, seek God, and make an objective decision. It is important that you make your decision based on God's ways, no matter what you decide. Every day, try to emulate God more, no matter your decision.

12

DOING MORE

And Moses quickly bowed down to the
ground and worshiped. He said, "If now I
have found favor in your sight, my Lord,
I pray, let my Lord go with us. Although
this is a stiff-necked people, pardon our
iniquity and our sin, and take us for your
inheritance."

Exodus 34:8-9

AFTER YOU HAVE REFLECTED on what we have discussed
in this book, what else might you do? What other response

might you have after dwelling upon God's ways, your identity, and God's people?

Worship

> And Moses quickly bowed down to the
> ground and worshiped.

Spend time in worship. This doesn't mean attending a worship service somewhere. Worship God in your tent of meeting. Worship God wherever you may be.

Sometimes, taking a breather from dwelling on our problems can be helpful. Worship is the best way to find rest.

One of the amazing things I find about worship is that it leaves me wanting more. After a good worship session, I am filled with the joy of the Lord. It inspires me. It seems the more I experience God in worship, the more I want of God. Singing about God's goodness and grace, meditating upon his great love, exalting his holy name, makes me want to do it more and more.

This is not about a distraction. It's not about getting your mind off your problems. Worship is about acknowledging the one who loves and cares for you. Worship is praising the deliverer of the past, present, and future.

Anne Graham Lotz makes an amazing observation about Daniel's prayer in Daniel 9. She points out that Daniel spends most of his prayer acknowledging God. Daniel worships God more than anything else.[1]

By following this book, you can praise the Lord without needing answers to your frustrations. You can worship God for his great love, knowledge, and care for you, your church, and the world.

As soon as God proclaimed his ways to Moses, Moses fell on his face and worshipped the Lord. Worship seems to be the natural reaction to talking with God. However you prefer to worship. Do so.

Ask for More

He said, "If now I have found favor in your sight, my Lord, I pray, let my Lord go with us.

---

1. Anne Graham Lotz. The Daniel Prayer: Prayer That Moves Heaven and Changes Nations (Grand Rapids: Zondervan, 2016).

Although this is a stiff-necked people,
pardon our iniquity and our sin, and take
us for your inheritance."

Asking for more is another option. After everything
we have discussed in the book, one would think we
have asked for enough. Don't be afraid to ask God
for more. If what you are asking is based upon God,
God's ways, and God's will, God will not get mad if you
request more. If you desire a deeper, richer, and fuller
relationship with God, God will not withhold it because
you can't get enough.

The Psalmist declared,

"God opens his hand, satisfying the desire of every
living thing. The Lord is near to all who call on him, to
all who call on him in truth. God fulfills the desire of all
who fear him; he also hears their cry and saves them. The
Lord watches over all who love him" (145:16, 18-20).

If you desire God, he will give you what you desire. If
you are calling on God because you want nothing else
but to serve him in pastoral leadership, God will be near
you. God will rush to your side. If you fear him, God
will hear your cry and save you.

Moses asked for three things as part of his worship. I suggest making these three things part of your request as well.

Be With Us

Ask God to be with you, and your church. You are part of them as much as they are part of you.

At the end of his conversation with God, Moses came to a place that he no longer asked for himself. Rather, he asked for his people. This seems to be a key transition in Moses' leadership. He no longer sees the people apart from himself. He is a part of them, and they are a part of him. In fact, Moses uses the term "us".

While it is important for God to be with you, for you to have a relationship with God, there is a difference when you can see with "us" lenses. When it is no longer something they did, but something that affects all, and you can approach God in this way, pastoral leadership takes on a different meaning. The focus shifts from anger, frustration, and bitterness to complete dependence upon God "from which our help comes." You see everything, good or bad, as an impact on God's people.

Resignation Sunday becomes about us, not just you. It is no longer a me versus them prayer. It is an "us" prayer. You start asking God how he would handle the us situation.

What's best for us? Its to tell God you are in it for the long haul. You are not going anywhere. Show me what to do by showing me you.

Forgive Us

Ask God to forgive your iniquity and sin—your sin and the church's. You seek forgiveness for your sin, acknowledging your shortcomings. You seek forgiveness for your people, including those that you may feel caused your turmoil. Ask forgiveness for everyone.

Moses knew all too well that his people were stiff-necked. He must have known his own bent to sinfulness as well. As he worshipped, Moses asked God to forgive "us". Once again, he sees himself as part of his people.

I can't help but recall the teaching of Jesus regarding judging others without judging yourself. Do not point out the speck in another's eye without removing the plank in your own first (Matthew 7:4).

Moses got it. Moses understood it wasn't just his people that needed forgiveness, he did as well.

Include yourself when praying for forgiveness. Often, it is not just your people that are acting against God's will, you are as well.

In my denomination, we often pray congregational confessions. When I first started praying these prayers, I felt offended. I hadn't done some things we were confessing. But as God broadened my understanding, I realized I was confessing for all humanity. I know that may sound strange to some. Yet, some of the greatest prayers in the Bible include such confessions. Daniel confessed on behalf of his nation. The Psalmist confessed on behalf of Israel. The prophets often spoke of Israel's sins, asking God to restore them as a people.

It's our sin that Christ died for. It is not just your sin or someone else's sin. The sins of humanity placed him there.

Don't stand apart from your people when asking for forgiveness. Stand amongst them, lifting your hands to God, asking God to forgive "us."

Take Us

Ask God to take you as his people, all of you. You are asking God to take you, the people you like, those you don't, and everyone else in your church as his.

One of the hardest lessons of Jesus to apply to our lives comes from Luke's Sermon on the Plain.

"But I say to you who are listening: Love your enemies; do good to those who hate you; bless those who curse you; pray for those who mistreat you. If anyone strikes you on the cheek, offer the other also, and from anyone who takes away your coat do not withhold even your shirt. Give to everyone who asks of you, and if anyone takes away what is yours, do not ask for it back again. Do to others as you would have them do to you.

"If you love those who love you, what credit is that to you? For even sinners love those who love them. If you do good to those who do good to you, what credit is that to you? For even sinners do the same. If you lend to those from whom you expect to receive payment, what credit is that to you? Even sinners lend to sinners, to receive as much again. Instead, love your enemies, do good, and lend, expecting nothing in return. Your reward will be great, and you will be children of the Most High, for he himself is kind to the ungrateful and the wicked. Be merciful, just as your Father is merciful (Luke 6: 27-38).

Can you ask God to take us as his people—all of us, those you like, and those who have hurt you or made you feel like quitting? Can you stand alongside those who have mistreated you, refused to hear God's Word, or acted sinfully, and ask God to take them, and you, as his people?

That's challenging. I know. Yet, in the words of the Master, this is who our Father is. This is what our Father does. He is kind to the ungrateful and the wicked.

As I have emphasized throughout this book, it's not enough to know God's ways except you follow his ways—become like him. This was the message of Jesus as well. God is merciful. Be merciful like your Father.

Ask God to take you and your people as his own.

13

RECEIVING MORE

As we come to the close of Moses' conversation with God, the Bible records three things that occur. I suggest these three things can occur for us as well.

Covenant

> He said, "I hereby make a covenant."
>
> Exodus 34:10

God made a covenant with the Israelites. God committed himself to the Israelites, calling them to observe his commands.

The Law, given by God a second time, underwent a rewriting process by Moses. Moses took the new ordinances back to the people, sharing it with them.

Even though stubbornness and rebellion persisted among the people, God's words still accompanied them. The people treasured God's words. They strived to follow them.

After receiving God's Law, the Israelites set out on their journey from Sinai to the Promised Land. Though the original descendants and Moses would not enter, God's people were becoming God's people, flaws and all.

You cannot make your people follow God, anymore than Moses could. But you can continue to call your people to follow God, just as Moses did. You can continue to lift up God's word and promises. You can hold hope before them, reminding them of their destination as God's people. The message doesn't change. God's love and faithfulness remain steadfast.

God has never abandoned his people or revoked his promises. We have no reason to think God will now.

The very message that you clung to when you first became a Christian is the same message you proclaim. Tell your people God loves them. Invite them to believe, love, and trust Jesus. As you do, let your life show them how.

Signs and Wonders

> Before all your people I will perform marvels,
> such as have not been done in all the earth or
> in any nation, and all the people among whom
> you live shall see the work of the Lord, for it is
> an awesome thing that I will do with you.
>
> Exodus 34:10

The second thing that occurred is the Israelites witnessed wonders and marvels in their midst. They routed their enemies without having to lift a hand. Nations knew the Israelites weren't like other nations. Greater nations feared them.

Their journey wasn't without setbacks. Yet, Israel saw great things. God's marvels were so profound that they are still talked about today. The Israelites were still writing songs and prayers about God's deliverance hundreds of years afterwards. When prophets lifted their voices to God, asking for deliverance yet again, they referred to the days of Moses. Even the New Testament church and the Apostles spoke of God's majestic deeds performed during the Exodus story.

Imagine if you led your people to stay on the journey, to keep moving looking for what wonders and marvels God will do. To declare to them as obstacles occur, as they will, that as people of God we don't look at the hinderances. Rather, we look at the possibilities of what God may do next. You see challenges as opportunities to point to God's ways, asking how do we act like God. By following God, you experience God in your midst.

Shining Leadership

> Moses came down from Mount Sinai. As
> he came down from the mountain with the
> two tablets of the covenant in his hand,
> Moses did not know that the skin of his face
> shone because he had been talking with God.
> When Aaron and all the Israelites saw Moses,
> the skin of his face was shining, and they

were afraid to come near him. But Moses
called to them, and Aaron and all the leaders
of the congregation returned to him, and
Moses spoke with them. Afterward all the
Israelites came near, and he gave them
in commandment all that the Lord had
spoken with him on Mount Sinai. When
Moses had finished speaking with them, he
put a veil on his face, but whenever Moses
went in before the Lord to speak with him,
he would take the veil off until he came
out, and when he came out and told the
Israelites what he had been commanded,
the Israelites would see the face of Moses,
that the skin of his face was shining, and
Moses would put the veil on his face again
until he went in to speak with him.

Exodus 34:29-35

Moses became a shining leader, symbolically and
literally. His face radiated from God's presence as he
came off the mountain after his encounter with God.
Afterward, when Moses went in and out of the Tent of
Meeting to spend time with God, his face glowed.

I had just been appointed to my very first church. As a rookie preacher, I was nervous, as you can imagine. I had spent days and weeks praying as I prepared to lead this church.

The first Sunday had arrived. I was delivering my first Children's Sermon as the children gathered around me at the front of the church. As I concluded the sermon, I distributed candy to each of the kids. Taking turns, each child reached into the candy bag, took a few pieces, and then returned to their parents.

The last child, a young boy, eased up to where I sat with the candy bag. Rather than reaching his hand into the bag, he stared at me intensely. He placed both hands on the side of my face and asked, "Are you Jesus?"

"No," I chuckled. "I'm not Jesus. I just work for him."

The boy's reply has inspired my ministry ever since he spoke it. I often weep thinking about it and when I try to share it.

"You look like Jesus," He said. "Your face shines so bright."

I can't tell you what that little boy really saw. I wouldn't dare say it had anything to do with my prayers. I will tell you God used that little boy's words prophetically. God was telling me what people should see in me. For God to be seen in me, I was going to have to spend time with God. For it is only in knowing God, God's ways, that others see God in me.

The words of Jesus' longest prayer recorded seem to apply here:

"As you, Father, are in me and I am in you, may they also be in us, so that the world may believe that you have sent me. The glory that you have given me I have given them, so that they may be one, as we are one, I in them and you in me, that they may become completely one, so that the world may know that you have sent me and have loved them even as you have loved me" (John 17:21-23).

Please listen to me, dear pastor. Whether or not you resign, make sure your people know you have been in the very presence of God. Let the radiance from your face testify the glorious power of the Living Lord. Don't tell them how much you have prayed, how often you have read your Bible, or how hard you have worked for the Kingdom. Show them. You let them see God in you.

It's interesting that Moses' conversation with God is bracketed by the Tent of Meeting. It begins by describing Moses going in and out of the Tent of Meeting to meet with God. After the covenant is renewed, and the story continues, it tells the story of Moses going in and out before the Lord once again.

Let no one accuse you of not spending time with God. They may say many things against you, false or true, but let the radiance of your life reveal you know God personally, speaking with him daily—many times a day.

14

IMAGINE

COVENANT, WONDERS, AND SHINING Leadership. Can these things occur to you? Can these result from you placing the resignation letter back into the drawer or perhaps shredding it?

Only God knows those answers. What you choose to do, however, may be the determining factor.

One thing is for certain. If you don't follow God's ways, you have no reason to expect anything other than what you are already experiencing.

Be like God, look to his ways to know your ways.

Be merciful.

Be gracious and slow to anger.

Allow the love of God in your heart to remain faithful despite your people.

Forgive.

Imagine if you rose from your desk, as one called to lead, known and favored by God, embracing God, and modeling the ways of God to your people. Imagine what might be.

Maybe your people will see God in you. Maybe they will follow as you hold up God's Word before them. Maybe they will obey, witnessing glorious things in their future. Maybe, just maybe, they too will make God's ways their own.

Thank you so much for reading Resignation Monday. If you haven't downloaded the special PrecisionFaith Devotional, Belief Made Simple: A Holy Week Journey into Discipleship, join the PrecisionFaith Newsletter at www.precisionfaith.com to get your free copy today. You can purchase a paperback version on Amazon as well.

Yes, reviews help get this book into the hands of others. If you know someone who this book could benefit, please leave a review.

Let's go make disciples!

Sincerely,

Toby Lofton

Take your pastoral leadership to the next level. Let the Apostle Paul's prayers teach you how to pray for your people. Get your copy of Praying for Your People: A Pastor's Guide every Christian Should Read. Available on Amazon and other retailers.

More books by Toby Lofton

PrecisionFaith Prayer Series

Jesus: 21 Days That Can Change the Way You Pray

Acts: Prayer That Can Change Your Church

Praying for Your People: A Pastor's Guide Every
Christian Should Read

Praying for Your Pastor: A Church Member's Guide
Every Pastor Should Read

PrecisionFaith Devotional Series

Spirituality Made Simple: An Advent Journey into
Spiritual Growth

Faith Made Simple: A Christmas Journey into Belief

Christ Made Simple: An Epiphany Journey into Identity

Discipleship Made Simple: A Lenten Journey into Following Jesus

Devotion Made Simple: An Easter Journey into Obedience

Mission Made Simple: A Pentecost Journey into Faith-Sharing

Other Books

Psalms of Sinner

Recognizing Jesus in Your Everyday Life

TOBY LOFTON

Dr. Toby Lofton is the Founder of PrecisionFaith, a platform that helps others to follow Jesus Christ. He is the author of the #1 Best-selling devotional, Jesus: 21 Days That Can Change the Way You Pray, and other books. His doctoral work created an Order that helped military chaplains recover, sustain, and strengthen their spirituality. Toby has over twenty-four years of church leadership and is a retired US Army Chaplain living in Mississippi with his wife. They have three adult children and six grandchildren.

You can find out more about Dr. Lofton and PrecisionFaith at www.precisionfaith.com.

A PrecisionFaith Devotional

BELIEF
MADE
SIMPLE

A HOLY WEEK JOURNEY
— INTO —
DISCIPLESHIP

TOBY LOFTON

Your Free Devotional Is Waiting

Searching for more meaning to Holy Week? Discover how
to enrichen your belief in the one who died for your sins.

*Get a free electronic copy of this special PrecisionFaith
Devotional honoring the last days of Christ.
Available for Kindle and e-readers, or PDF at*
https://dl.bookfunnel.com/deanxe7n16.
Purchase a paperback version on Amazon.

www.precisionfaith.com

Discover more books from Toby and subscribe for free to receive weekly encouragement and Christian articles.

Made in the USA
Middletown, DE
10 April 2025

74077116R00088